The Study Abroad Truth:

You might just discover yourself

Connor LaVallie and Sean O'Bryan

"Travel is fatal to prejudice, bigotry, and narrow-mindedness, and many of our people need it sorely on these accounts. Broad, wholesome, charitable views of men and things cannot be acquired by vegetating in one little corner of the earth all one's lifetime."

— Mark Twain, *The Innocents Abroad/ Roughing It*

THIS BOOK IS DEDICATED TO YOU, THE
STUDENT, AND ALL THOSE WHO HELPED US
REALIZE THE *TRUTH* IN STUDYING ABROAD.

ACKNOWLEDGMENTS

This book would not have been possible without the wisdom and guidance of many people in our corners. We would like to thank our families for all their love and support. Especially our parents, AJ and Erin LaVallie, Dennis and Mary Ellen O'Bryan ~ we love you very much. Connor would also like to thank his grandparents, Mike and Maralyn Reilly.

Thank you Meghan Eaves, for your research and valuable advice, Loyola University Chicago, Fr. Michael Garanzini, Emilio Iodice, Colleen Calvey, Paula DeVoto, Todd Waller, Nicholas Scimeca, Van Tu, Roger O'Bryan, Fr. Mark Bosco, Kate Patterson, Per Ellingson, Jack Eisenberg, Mike Brennan, Kerry Logan, Mariam Pera, Bethany Dockins, Amelia Blanton, Lys Zawalski, Bob Cannell, and countless others who shared in our adventures and helped us along the way. We are grateful for you all.

TABLE OF CONTENTS

Foreword
From two people we respect most

"Say *yes* to *everything*... as long as it's not stupid or illegal". Embarrassingly, that was the final piece of fatherly advice I left my son with as we shook hands in the International Terminal at Chicago's O'Hare airport. His mother would have liked to be there but she knew she would cry. Having not demonstrated a predisposition towards being outwardly social or particularly a risk taker I thought it was good advice for him for the next one hundred days. Naively these were my flawed preconceived notions about my son that were and are, by their very nature as his father, preconceived and flawed. It didn't take him long to begin to open my eyes to the infinite possibilities that stood before him in the true dawn of his adult life. In fact, his second weekend of "study abroad" was a side trip to Switzerland that included skydiving and snowboarding over the snow covered Swiss Alps in January. When we received the videotaped CD in the mail from him 3 weeks later I wanted to retract my bon voyage advice! But it was too late... he was on his way to something truly extraordinary... something that would change him forever!

Getting out of your comfort zone is not only good advice for studying abroad... it is the very essence of it. You can't be willing to study abroad and expect it to be just like home. In many ways it is the antithesis of being at home. But the opportunity, the potential for enlightenment and growth, the chance to really learn as much about yourself as you do the rest of the world is~true poetry. Oh for the road less traveled, or better yet... for the road almost NOT traveled because it appeared too challenging, but then was taken just the same. If you're going to go for it, it needs to be done right, in the right program and with the right forethought... but the benefits will truly last a lifetime.

Life is not a destination. Life's a journey ~ enjoy the ride!

A.J. LaVallie, CFP

When I was growing up in the 50's and 60's, a common saying by my parents was that they wanted their kids to do better than they did, not with regard to morals but regarding quality of life matters, such as income, leisure, travel, etc.

I can say that with regard to my son Sean, I have definitely succeeded as it relates to that 1950's notion insofar as through his high school sponsored travel abroad programs, and collegiate study abroad programs, he has definitely traveled and visited more countries than I have.

The worldly perspective he has acquired is self-evident throughout this book. Being immersed and exposed to various cultures around the world has imbued in him a life perspective that is not usually acquired by others less traveled. While the expense of studying abroad is not negligible, the life experience acquired is worth it.

If I had to pick what I think is the most important part of his dissertation it would be that concerning not partying your study abroad trip away, but going outside the box and experiencing it. In fact, I would say that is a lesson for one's entire life.

Dennis O'Bryan, J.D.

Introduction

Should you study abroad?

You can talk to counselors, teachers, and administrators. You can read tons of brochures. But right here in this book you can get the firsthand account from several study abroad students who did it, and loved every minute of it. Well, almost every minute. Our names are Connor and Sean. I (Connor) graduated with a B.S. degree in Psychology from Loyola University Chicago in 2010 and am now completing graduate studies in Chiropractic and Naturopathic medicine. I will be relaying to you my experiences in chapters one through nine. I (Sean) graduated with a B.B.A. in Finance and Marketing from Loyola University Chicago in 2010 and am now pursuing J.D. and M.B.A. degrees. I will be sharing my experiences in chapters ten through twelve.

Ever since we started college, we had been debating with ourselves about whether or not we should study abroad. We didn't talk about it much with friends or family because we were a little apprehensive about the whole idea at first. We were excited about living in a place so different from home because of the places we'd see, people we'd meet, and challenges we'd strive to overcome. However, making this decision was definitely not an easy one.

Just like many of you, we were quite nervous just thinking about all the uncertainties that lay before us. We found ourselves thinking about all the reasons why we should NOT study abroad. We thought about missing our families and friends. We worried about all the planning, paperwork, and potential obstacles we would have to go through. We couldn't help but think about risks involved, safety issues, language limitations, finding decent food, maintaining some level of comfort, and of course... paying for all of it. Additionally, we wondered if we would be able to graduate on time. Would the right courses be available? And would it all be worth it in the end? Back then we were searching for information that would settle our nerves, but we didn't get many answers we were happy with.

That's when we decided to do our own investigation. We talked with dozens of former college students from different parts of the world, and asked them what they wished they had done differently throughout college. To our surprise, an astonishing 8 out of 10 graduates said they regretted not studying abroad! As we talked, it was apparent we shared all the same concerns- language, curriculum, personal safety and well-being. However we still had the opportunity in front of us, they did not.

Connor: In the first chapter, I will discuss why my decision became clear to study abroad that spring. If you are interested in making the most of your time, I believe you will relate to my story. However I hope you will develop your own reasons, and begin to understand the potential rewards that await you. I was not always prepared for everything at the time, I was not able to gather all the information I could possibly need, and sometimes I paid for it. All in all, the months I spent studying overseas became the most fun, gratifying, and educational times I could ever have imagined. Making that choice to leave became a decision that has ultimately shaped my character for the better in so many ways, and I know it will do the same for you... if you do it right! I also believe you will continue to discover the full benefits of the whole experience, and the positive ways they've affected you for many years to come.

Don't miss the opportunity

Motivated by our newfound knowledge, we decided to dig deeper and get to the bottom of why so many students had failed to make the decision to go. When we thought about how valuable this experience was, we realized it was a shame that more students didn't seize this opportunity. Maybe their choice would have been a lot easier had they known more about the uncertainties ahead, logistical concerns, ways to finance the trips, things to avoid, tips for getting around, and how to make the most of the entire experience. **That is why we wrote this book: to offer students like you the benefit of our experience. We want to help you make your decision to study abroad, and get the most from it. This book covers what you need to do: before leaving, during your stay, and as a bonus, special ways to apply your experience back home.** It's not only about our personal journey. We interviewed other students so you'll get their advice as well. They will share some secrets about how to avoid making mistakes, and what you should *really* know when it comes to studying overseas.

When you return, you will find yourself utilizing the lessons you've learned in everyday life. We know, because we are still using them to this day on ourselves. Studying abroad will expand your worldview, help you develop *more* confidence in yourself, and bring you closer to friends both old and new. If you make the jump, commit yourself to leaving home, and delve into the unknown for a while ... there are tremendous opportunities that await you. After reading this book, we are confident you will see that the possibilities are truly endless!

You will get to hear about particular trips we took at the beginning of each chapter, and by the end you will have all the information you need to not only "get through" your months overseas ... but truly *MAXIMIZE YOUR STUDY ABROAD*. Each story takes place in one of the cities we visited while studying abroad. We hope this will give you a fresh perspective, and help you think about some of the places you'll want to visit when your time comes. In the meantime, sit back and relax while we tell you the *Truth* about studying abroad!

1. How I Made the Decision; it wasn't easy

Loyola University Chicago- "Preparing People to Lead Extraordinary Lives"

Scurrying through the narrow corridors of the slippery, dusty lecture halls at my institution abroad, I couldn't help but stop and read the promising quote painted on the wall. It was written in large maroon and gold letters throughout campus-

"Preparing People to Lead Extraordinary Lives" I looked up and repeated it to myself many times during the semester. For me, this statement started out as just an overly optimistic sentiment. In fact, my attitudes about it would change as often as the weather in my hometown, Chicago. However, after living here at the John Felice Rome Center for the past few months, my outlook has evolved. I started to believe that these words carried some substance and meaning. This belief was slowly becoming a conviction, and I *knew* it would be a promise to those of us living here in Rome, Italy. I talked with some of my closest friends and they agreed that their outlook had also changed. We were definitely being prepared to live extraordinary lives. How did our views about our school's motto change so quickly? To understand this, I have to look back at what was happening before I decided to study abroad.

Back to the beginning

When I was a freshman, my father and I talked extensively about my future plans in school. Just like many of you, I found comfort in discussing everything from sports and relationships, to graduate school and my potential career with someone I could trust. That someone was my dad. Anytime I sit down and talk with him, we usually have conversations that evoke new insight and clarity about any issue we tackle. I am extremely fortunate to have a supportive family that fosters an environment where all mistakes are accepted as 'lessons learned' rather than punishment. My dad and I always come away from our discussions having discovered something new and valuable from each other. When we started exploring some of the potential options I had, we were most excited about the opportunity to study abroad.

He immediately suggested going to Loyola's Beijing Center in the heart of China. I thought it sounded incredible, but I wanted to do a little more research before I committed. After my freshman year, I received an invitation to apply for a scholar program which involved living abroad for a whole year. The fall semester would be in Rome where I would begin a research project, and then finish it up during the spring semester in Beijing. I wanted a challenge, and living in both cities for a whole year sounded like an incredible test. However, at the beginning of my sophomore year I changed my major, which ultimately affected my eligibility to be a part of the research program. I was especially disappointed when I heard this new because I had just told my grandparents about my plans. My grandfather even said he was going to start looking for flights so they could come out to visit me. Telling them I wasn't going anymore was difficult, but I also said they would be the first to know if I ever found the right program.

Time to make some moves

As an upperclassman in college, I realized time was slipping by quickly. I knew I was at a unique stage in my life, and the great leap to adulthood was approaching rapidly. Up until this point I was content with finding competitive outlets, new hobbies, great friends, and teachers. However I knew deep down there was something missing. I had a choice though. I was fortunate enough to have certain options most people in the world wouldn't even consider possible, and they were right there in front of me. I just needed to muster up the courage to grab them. I had to explore.

My dad's voice echoed in my head "this is a small window of opportunity you have to try new things, experience something unique ... get a little uncomfortable for a while" I had heard this repeatedly, and I had grown somewhat tired of it. Although I knew it was true. I decided that studying abroad would be the single best way to "try something new and get uncomfortable for a while."

I talked with some of my older friends about why they didn't study abroad. Most of them said they wanted to, but they never made the commitment because they told themselves it would "just happen someday" or they would "hopefully go abroad after school at some point". Of course it never happened, and they expressed their regret. One guy in particular tried to justify his decision when he told me "well, there are no good gyms outside the U.S., and the food is horrible!" I decided this was his opinion, and he was probably correct to some degree, but I still needed to hear more.

Finals week was approaching. As a result, I found myself in a cluttered state of exhaustion at the end of almost every day leading up to my exams. The continuous months of perusing scientific journals, writing poetry, exploring the inner conflicts of Islam, blogging about new media, and debating about all the various alternative energy sources was common at a Jesuit institution. I was becoming a well-rounded student! What an outstanding place to learn and prepare for real life. Yes, of course I thought... but after a few mundane weeks of perpetual studying, I became envious of the janitor cleaning my desk.

Gaining insights from a friend

That night my roommate Sean and I were finishing up a workout at the school's recreational center. Between a couple sets on the incline bench, we asked one another whether or not we had thought about studying abroad. Sean expressed his apprehensions about maintaining his lifestyle in a place so different from the United States. However he also said "we do have to consider the incredible perspective we would gain by stepping outside our comfort zones in another country... it would be challenging". Even though his response was very motivational speaker-like, I thought it was an awesome insight. I was a little worried about becoming acclimated to traditions and customs so different from my own for so long. But the thought of leaving our "comfort zones" is what stuck out to me most. I thought of the old adage "If you do what you've always done, you'll get what you've always got" and "true character is only shaped in the absence of comfort". I knew I had been "comfortable" for too long and if I didn't force a change now, it might never happen.

We decided it would be worth the risks, and anything we missed at home would be minuscule in comparison to the pain of regret. A former student told me "The most important thing to do is just to make the right decision for YOU; don't worry about having a best friend or familiar face to tag along with." Based on this distinction, I did not think it was critical to find a congenial roommate or travel partner, but I did anyway. If I hadn't though, I knew that all of us students would be in the same situation with similar worries. This would bring us closer, and there would be many opportunities to make new friends abroad.

Start Paying Attention

As I was leaving the Halas sports center to get a bite to eat, I noticed a flyer posted next to the entrance that read "Study Abroad Information session meets today at 3 o'clock in the auditorium" I looked at my watch ... that was in twenty minutes! I couldn't believe I hadn't seen this earlier. I stood there and stared at the bright neon-green invitation while thinking of all the reasons about why I shouldn't go now ... "I can just e-mail the presenters" "I could ask my friends about it" "I have to study for my exams!" and "I still need to eat something" all of these thoughts were true, but I decided I would need to start making some small sacrifices if I wanted the privilege to study overseas for four months.

I arrived about two minutes early and busted through the auditorium doors with my notebook in hand. I was ready to soak in stories, tips, warnings, and anything else these presenters decided would be useful for someone like me.

I sat there anxiously; watching as other excited and scared looking students filed into rows like it was some type of rock concert. I was not expecting so much enthusiasm since we were in the midst of finals week, but this was clearly something special. I sat there quietly while scanning the room and looking for a pen to jot down anything useful. There was a tension in the air. I was so distracted and excited by the thoughts of traveling abroad; I didn't even notice my roommate had come in. We obviously hadn't discussed anything about this meeting, and I knew communication would be crucial while studying abroad. I took my first note: "keep your eyes open and start talking, or this will be a lot harder than it needs to be". Sean was sitting about ten rows up. He was joking with someone in a seemingly ultra relaxed type of way, which was not really my forte. We were so different I thought; how could I ever get along with someone like this for four months overseas?

Just as my intense, type-A thoughts about leaving really started to race; a tall, thin, silver-haired Italian woman with thick-rimmed glasses stormed into the auditorium. Her green blazer, white blouse, and long red and white skirt looked like an Italian flag under the bright stage lights.

Her voice boomed over the loud speaker "Studenti benvenuti! I'm Paula, your program director and I will be talking with you about some of the things you'll need in order to survive Rome next semester!" Survive? I thought... awesome. This sounded like more than an adventure. I began to understand that it would be impossible to do any of this "halfway"... It was all or nothing now.

I began scribbling down everything I thought I would need ... warm clothes (*especially if we plan on sleeping in the Sahara desert...?*), towels, at least sixteen weeks worth of clothing, laptop (with a lock, key, and Skype), *don't buy school supplies... we could buy it there!?* Laundry essentials, hangers, digital camera(s) with plastic bags to prevent sand damage, journal, dictionaries (*in any language we plan on using*), driver's license with two copies, credit cards with two copies, debit cards with two copies, international airline ticket with the whole group, four copies of our passports (every page), an additional sixteen passport photos, phone cards, at least five hundred Euros, and... of course... a study visa.

My list was pretty decent since I copied down *everything* that was delivered in the presentation. However I spent more time trying to mentally project myself across the Atlantic. I thought about traveling to eccentric places, sampling local cuisine, getting lost in the piazzas, bargaining for strange souvenirs, making new friends, and most of all... trying not to get injured or killed while I was gone. After all, I had just signed the liability waiver. I was traveling the world at my own risk, and it was very real.

I was departing from my home, but I was also venturing off a beaten path it seemed. The traditional mold I had been thrust into when I was eighteen was starting to deteriorate. I knew this would be very different from the school I had grown to love back home. I trudged down the dim, vacant hallway outside the auditorium to find a place to rest, and *think*.

It's up to you

After attending these presentations, I knew for certain that there would never be a better time in my life to travel, live, and study overseas. After finally accepting this reality, I decided then and there that I would make the most of every moment I had abroad. However, the most critical thing to remember is this: Don't expect anyone to *hold your hand* through any of this. Your program directors will probably introduce you to the plethora of resources that can be utilized at your school, but don't be passive. Never make assumptions about requirements, deadlines, paperwork, or anything inherently critical to your admittance. Be proactive and plan ahead with your advisor in order to avoid any unexpected surprises!

Back when I was a freshman, I was disappointed that I couldn't become part of the scholar program. However I decided I wouldn't let that stop me. So what? I didn't get my first choice of programs. If this happens to you, don't allow it to affect your decisions. There are plenty of outstanding options available... the choice you make should be for *you* and no one else.

It has been said that studying abroad is an experience that broadens the mind, enhances the memory, and enlivens the soul. To get the most out of the experience, you should take the time to prepare properly and do a bit of research on your destination. By being adequately prepared, and ready to embrace the culture, you will be more likely to have a positive and memorable time abroad.

2. Getting Ready to Leave

Journal Entry- Pre Departure Reflection:

My original day of departure was supposed to be yesterday, January 7th. My scheduled flight was cancelled due to a snowstorm in Milan... oh here we go, great start I thought. Here it was a beautiful January day in Chicago, but the weather was violent in Italy. I was learning that the entire universe doesn't revolve around my little corner of the world. So my dad and I drove once again to the airport to begin the journey that would cap off my junior year in college at Loyola. I would be based in the *Eternal City*. Rome, a place praised by many near and far. People I've never met, and those I've known my entire life were changed significantly in one way or another after visiting this place. I will have approximately four months in Italy and other parts of world to discover what it's like to live amongst the locals.

Personally, I am a homebody at heart. I value family and take comfort knowing what will come at the conclusion of my day, or when I wake each morning. No matter where I go, no matter how long I'm gone, home is usually calling.

My eagerness to depart from this place, and live in Europe is due to my agitation with being *too* comfortable here. I must force myself to break free from this methodical environment I've constructed at home. When placed in unfamiliar territory, I find that it's normal to constantly introspect. Our senses sharpen, survival instincts start to kick in, and it becomes easier to let go of any of the senseless neurotic tendencies we have. This could give us a new perspective on life, and I hope to articulate some of the positive insights I gain when I return.

In America we're shaped by a culture of excess, competition, advantage, and freedom... our reality becomes exciting, yet somewhat predictable. A façade of confidence and pride lingers in many of Uncle Sam's young relatives I believe. That is until we actually stop and take a look around. Branching out can make us feel like fish out of water... like we're walking on eggshells. However we'll soon realize how isolated we were living within these borders.

Most of us would like to look back on our lives and know that we took advantage of the moments we've had... even if they were a direct violation of certain values like comfort, and proximity to family. I know my generation must take it upon itself to grow up in our delayed-age society where people live with their parents through college or long afterwards. Comfort can sometimes become our worst enemy. It can feel fantastic in the moment, but it will slowly diminish our true potential. We are like frogs in a pot of warm water. It feels good at first, but as time goes by, the heat slowly climbs and we eventually realize we need to get out or we'll die. Perhaps we won't boil to death like the frog, but we will certainly die emotionally when we decide it's good enough when things are just "OK" in life. Comfort is the silent killer, and sometimes we have to take a conscious, relentless pursuit of our own independence before it's too late.

I'm sitting at home now; waiting to drive to the airport again after my flight to Milan was cancelled yesterday due to heavy snowfall. I'm anxious, but I know it's now or never. I must harness the courage. I have my whole life to return to what I love doing, now is the time to become a better individual and do what doesn't feel right. I will see you abroad...
January 8.

How to prepare before departure

Studying abroad can be an intense mental experience. Before you go, you will want to spend some time ensuring that you are mentally prepared for your trip so that you can cut down on culture shock and spend more time enjoying your days oversees.

Believe it or not, one of the most exciting times in your entire study abroad experience is the few months and weeks before your departure. You feel like everything is a great big unknown, waiting to be discovered. Your mind races with thoughts of what life overseas will be like, how you will handle it, what kinds of friends you'll make, and which incredible places you'll see. However, this is probably the time that most study abroad students take for granted.

(While preparing to leave, check out www.goabroad.com for some useful information about some of the unique opportunities available to you)

In the weeks prior to your trip, gather your thoughts and enjoy your home. Spend time thinking about what you'll want to accomplish before you leave. Make sure to allow yourself plenty of space and hours to plan, shop, and pack. Rushing through packing is the last thing you want. If you do, it can be very easy to forget the small, but important items. However you will be able to find most of the things you'll need overseas, so don't worry if you forget something.

You're probably wondering what you should pack and how to prepare. Starting from about the six-month mark before you leave, you need to begin preparing. Seriously, six months might seem like a long time in advance, but believe me, once you get into the groove of planning your trip, you'll be grateful for all those extra days.

Start by preparing yourself for many atypical experiences. Be mentally ready to eat foods you don't recognize, try social activities that are new, and go to destinations (museums, discotecas, etc.) that might not appeal to you in the states. You may even want to start looking into certain travel destinations you *know* you're going to want to visit while abroad (Start now by checking out www.RyanAir.com and www.HostelWorld.com for great flight and lodging deals).

Planning in advance will also save you a lot of money, especially on plane tickets. Purchasing airfare ahead of time is likely to be cheaper, and it will give you time to build up your own savings account. You can book most hostels without a lot of advanced notice, but it might be helpful to scout out ratings, prices, and availability ahead of time just in case (Just visit www.HostelWorld.com and choose your destination. From there you will have no trouble finding the right place to stay). Trust me, those spontaneous events like sampling all the delicious local foods, and taking weekend trips will be tempting. Finding these deals early will allow you more freedom to experience whatever you want once you arrive without blowing your savings.

Passports

If you don't already have one, the first thing you need to get is your **passport**. This is an ID document that allows you to travel internationally. Inside, it has your picture and lots of pages for stamps and visas for all the countries you plan to visit. It also has a special chip inside that can be read by computers at every immigration counter around the world. This means that there are electronic records of you traveling between countries, which is absolutely necessary for your own protection.

It's critical that you have these documents in order before you leave. It can be quite inconvenient to be abroad without these things done properly. Even though dealing with paperwork and logistics is not a lot of fun, you will be saving yourself a lot trouble. Spend time with the paperwork *before you leave* so you can focus on what's really important~~making the most of your precious time.

It is shocking how few Americans actually have their passports, considering how easy they are to get. To apply for your passport, you should start by visiting http://travel.state.gov and clicking on the "Passports" tab at the top of the page. Here, you can complete the application form (DS-11) and download and print it.

Once you've filled out your application, you need to collect a few things before applying in person at your local post office branch (check your post office's website to find the nearest branch that accepts passport applications)

Here is a short list of the things you'll need:

- ❑ Form DS-11, filled out and left **unsigned** (you'll sign it when you apply)
- ❑ Evidence of U.S. citizenship - birth certificate or naturalization certificate
- ❑ ID - driver's license or other government photo ID
- ❑ Photocopy of ID - Xerox copy of the front and back of your ID on plain, white 8 ½ x 11 paper
- ❑ Application fee - by check, money order or bank draft (no cash or credit)
- ❑ Multiple color passport photos - you can have these taken at pharmacies, AAA offices and travel agencies. If you wear glasses, keep them on for the photo. These photos are used abroad for student ids, bus passes, and a host of other official purposes, so having 4 – 6 of these on hand when you arrive can save a good deal of time and expense on the ground.

❑ Social Security Card

A regular adult passport cost $100 and can take up
to 6 weeks to arrive, so it's **very important** that you
apply for your passport **as soon as you decide to
study abroad**.

Visas

A **visa** is a travel document that allows you to legally
enter a foreign country. There are many different
types of visas. You will find them ranging from
tourist visas to permanent residence permits.
Additionally, each country has its own set of rules
and regulations for who is required to get a visa, and
which types of visas are available. If you've ever
traveled abroad before and received a stamp inside
your passport, this is a kind of visa ~ a tourist stamp
issued on the spot to allow you to enter the country.

In most countries, study abroad students are
provided with some kind of student visa. Whether or
not you're required to apply in advance depends on
where you're going to be studying. For example, in
Ireland, non-European study abroad students can
enter the country without obtaining a visa
beforehand. However they must register as students
with the local immigration authority after they arrive.
Conversely, students studying in China must present

their passports at a Chinese embassy to get their official visa in the United States before they leave. Similarly, Italy and most other countries require a visa pre-departure as well.

Finding out what the visa requirements are for your chosen study abroad country isn't too difficult. Follow these steps:

1) If you are going abroad through an **official study abroad program** at your high school or university, contact the study abroad or international office. They can provide you with the details about what type of visa you will need for your trip.

2) If you are studying through a **private study abroad program**, contact the program administrator for details about what specific type of visa you will need. This will usually depend on your living arrangements, and the duration of your stay.

3) If you are studying abroad **independently** or doing **graduate work** abroad, contact the international office at the university or college abroad where you'll be studying. They are your best source for advice about the visa you'll need.

4) If all else fails, check the website of [insert your study abroad country here]'s embassy in the United States for details on obtaining a student visa. No matter what, it is not a difficult process so don't fret. The groups mentioned above should be able to provide all the support you'll need to obtain your visa.

In some cases, you may be asked to send your passport to the embassy by mail. If you don't live close to the embassy you need, you might have to enlist the help of a **visa service.** You can apply online for a visa service in your area, and a representative will take your passport to the embassy of your destination country. It is their job to obtain a visa on your behalf so you can concentrate on learning more about the country you will soon be living in.

Pre-departure homework

Now that you've taken care of getting your passport and visa, you'll want to start doing some homework about the country that you've chosen. More than likely, you picked this place because it has some particular interest to you. Perhaps you want to explore your family's ancestral roots, maybe you've been studying French and want to try living in France, or maybe you've always been interested in

Chinese kung fu, so you're headed to Shanghai for a semester.

No matter how familiar you are with the country, you will need to do some *more* homework to find out about what to expect. Even if you think you know everything there is to know, you're wrong. But that's part of the fun. Keep exploring! If you're going abroad through your university's official program, they've probably already provided you some pamphlets or a reading list to get you started.

Head to Barnes & Noble on a scouting trip. You'll obviously want to check out the "Travel" sections, but also visit the "History" aisles for books about your chosen country. You might also want to invest in a **phrasebook**, especially if you don't have much experience with the language. And remember, even if you *have been* studying the language, using it everyday with native speakers is going to be incredibly different from using it in a classroom. You will find that your phrasebook will bring many benefits throughout your journey. Obtaining a great **map** of the city where you'll be living is also a fantastic idea. Guidebooks like *Lonely Planet* or *Rough Guides* are a smart place to start for basic travel and culture information about your country of choice.

Make sure to read up on the culture and customs of your chosen country, and spend some time thinking about how they might differ from your own. Think about the things that you *need* to make you feel somewhat comfortable everyday. However I'm not talking about ridding yourself of every possible challenge by taking along all the comforts of home. Doing this will only produce more stress and limit your potential growth while you're abroad. Just find that one thing you need, and if it's easy to carry... then you should definitely bring it along.

Before you leave, you should understand what your current limits are in terms of adapting to change. You'll spend most of your study abroad days far away from your personal comfort zone, and these limits will start to expand. Have your journal, music, family photo... *or whatever* on hand for some peace of mind.

Prepare yourself for the fact that some of your favorite stuff at home might not be readily available in your chosen country. Remember, that is one of the best things about studying abroad. You will probably realize some of your previous "needs" like television will become obsolete. Embrace your new environment and welcome the daily challenges it brings.

Living overseas isn't horribly difficult. Naturally, you'll just have to do some adjusting. Billions of people live in these same places with total satisfaction, so you can do it too. You are studying abroad to try exciting new things, test out life in a completely different way... and on a totally different level. If you can accept these facts, it's going to be an extremely educational and unforgettable time in your life.

Part of the *Truth* is you will discover that once you arrive, your willingness to face challenges and uncomfortable situations will increase considerably. This is because you will start to feel the satisfaction that comes from owning these challenges and facing your fears. So don't be afraid of living without anything you think you may need from home, you'll be getting stronger every day in their absence.

Where will you be living?

Thinking about **where to live** is something that weighs heavily on most study abroad students. Hopefully, you're enrolled through your home institution and will be provided with on-campus or **student housing**. Check with the study abroad office for more information, and remember that sometimes you must reserve living space for several months in advance.

If you're going independently, you'll need to start looking for an **apartment** or **room** at least a month ahead of time. Checking local apartment-finding websites and roommate sites can be a good place to start. In a lot of countries, especially in Europe, it is not uncommon for strangers to share a large house together. This can also be a great introduction to the local culture, as well as a quick way to make friends.

Student dorms and shared student housing are a common living arrangement for many study abroad journeys. To minimize any additional stress, prepare in advance for shared facilities. Naturally, you will be expected to share bathrooms and kitchen facilities with the other student's responsibly. Keep your things neat and understand that you will be expected to do your share of the cleaning and chores. In order to make the most of your experience in these conditions: Talk to your roommate. Communication is the key to any positive relationship; you guys will figure anything out as long as you are open with each other.

Before going in, understand that it may be louder in the overseas housing than what you are used to back home. There will not be a group of Resident Assistants patrolling floors like there are in many American colleges and other western universities. Be prepared for noise. If this is a problem, you can bring earplugs to help you get to sleep. Or better yet, you can join in the festivities. After all, studying abroad is about doing things a little bit differently than you would back at home.

In other places, such as South America or China, you might consider doing a **home stay**, where you live with a local family. These can be arranged on your own with the help of programs like AFS International. (*You can go to their website http:// www.afsusa.org for support on finding the best program for you*) Another great option is to check with the school or college where you'll be studying. They usually have lists of local families or apartments that are willing to welcome foreign students to their home. This can be an outstanding way to really learn about the culture, and make a lifelong connection.

If you're prepared to be respectful and accommodating with your host family, you should not have any trouble. However there are a few things you should think about before you leave. Primarily, you will need to be mindful of the house rules. This can include everything from chores and meal times to fulfilling all the expectations about family events. Remember to be polite at all times, even if you would prefer not to eat a certain item for dinner or if you don't like the fact that your host mother wants you home by a certain time. I suggest finding that "middle ground" with your host parents and understand that you can go back to doing anything you want *after* you return home. Most host families will be very flexible and welcoming to you, so it is only fair that you make a few sacrifices to ensure a peaceful living experience with them. Just remember to keep an open mind and be adaptable.

When it comes to studying abroad and living with a local family, there is no one I know who could provide a better insight than my friend Per. As early as he could remember, Per has grown up in the United States alongside students from all over the world. His parents have been hosting study abroad students for years, and Per got a chance to witness what a positive experience this could be for them. Therefore, he decided to study in Chile, South America with a native family for an entire year during high school. Below, Per will share his experience as an American student, and what it was like finding a new family overseas.

Living With a Family in Chile, South America

Until I was 16 years old, I only had one family.

After getting to know a number of exchange students from other countries in the United States, I made the decision to study abroad in high school. So, I filled out an application, and halfway through my sophomore year, I left my normal life in Downers Grove, Illinois, to spend 11 months in the small city of Los Angeles, Chile.

At the time, I knew a few things about the world, but not too much about what to expect. Latino culture in South America seemed inherently 'cooler' than the United States. I anxiously looked forward to the relaxed drinking age, and guessed that living in the US was thus innately inferior. I looked forward to picking up a second language, becoming more independent, and traveling, as well as escaping my life and my responsibilities at home. I already had these expectations in mind, but there were some things I gained from my experience that I could not have predicted.

As I stepped off the bus in Chile, my host family and I immediately met each other and I was greeted with warm hugs and kisses on the cheek. Much of the middle class in Los Angeles, Chile lives in tight cookie-cutter houses not far from the center of town. However my upper-middle class host family lived in a beautiful home on a spacious lot on the edge of town. When we pulled into their driveway, I noticed a sign attached to the front of the house with my name on it and the words "Bienvenidos a tu nuevo hogar" ("Welcome to your new home"). They were a happy family of four, and they took me in as their own. Little did I know at the time that I would become so attached to these four people in the eleven months that followed.

Daniel, my brother, Dani, mi hermano and I became close brotherly companions. Despite the availability of an extra bedroom in the house, Daniel and I chose to share a room for the extent of my stay. Even though he was twelve and I was sixteen when I first arrived, we began to do everything together. We would venture into town and travel to different villages and cities together. He introduced me to all of his friends and they accepted me with open arms. I was really beginning to like this place!

Daniel and I would come up with our own games or competitions all the time. We would kick the soccer ball around the back yard for hours at a time. When the weather was warm, instead of showering, we'd often just jump in the swimming pool. We'd stay up until the wee hours of the morning playing FIFA 2000 or Zelda on the Gamecube. One of our favorite movies was the Matrix, and we would often watch, discuss, and reenact our favorite scenes together. We shared experiences of mischief and misfortune, and created our own experiences together.

Mariela Pia, my sister, Marielita (little Mariela) was affectionately known among the family as "Gordy", which is short for "gordita" ("fatty") because she was pudgy until she grew out of infancy. Gordy and I fostered a strong relationship as older brother and younger sister. She was only ten years old when I went to Chile for the first time, and she was the sweetest thing on the planet. She was always hugging my waist or neck or arm. I became her defender from Daniel's brotherly bullying. I would give her piggyback rides all around the house. When I would make an embarrassing cultural blunder, she would publicly correct me with the matter-of-fact-ness that only a child could shamelessly do. As she has grown up, she has been modest about having a blue-eyed American big brother that her teenage classmates regard like a celebrity.

Pedro Igor, my father, (*Papá, Papito*) is the

workingman. His life is focused on providing for his family, and I'm filled with nothing but respect and admiration for him. As a doctor on call, he is always working... and he works hard. He was sometimes the most difficult to understand while I was trying to learn Chilean Spanish. His speech was very quick which left me scrambling to try and assemble the consonants that flashed past my ears. However he is very well spoken, humble, and dignified. He has always been one to tell me clearly and directly how things should be done there. He once prohibited me from continuing to wear a certain shirt because the ends of the sleeve were old, tattered, and coming apart. I still liked the shirt, but I listened to what he said.

Mariela, my mother (*Mamá, Mamita*) was the caretaker of us all. She would drive us to and from school early in the morning. She would take us to the mall, friends' houses, parties, and dance clubs late at night. On late mornings, we always snuggled up to her in the parents' big bed to eat breakfast and read together. She would ask, "What do you want for breakfast, my son?" and call down through the intercom to the maid room to put in our order of cereal, eggs with cheese, avocado, and juice. She soon began to care about me as deeply as her two biological children. We would run errands with her, and she would sometimes boast facetiously, yet proudly that I am her son during small talk with acquaintances in the chocolate shop, in the beauty shop, or in the Laundromat. By the time I left, my Spanish was good enough that I could have been passed off as her son!

To many, I was just a traveler, an exchange student, a foreign acquaintance, or a white stranger on the street. To others, I was a classmate, a friend, a soccer teammate, or an English tutor. But to my host family, I was much more. I spent a lot of time at school, playing soccer or music, and making friends. However I always went home to my Chilean family. We ate many meals together, made our own trips together, celebrated birthdays and holidays ... and simply lived together while building memories for a lifetime. None of us were surprised when they took me to the airport to return home at the end of the year, but we all wept uncontrollably. After just eleven months, we were family, and we didn't want to separate.

In the end I realized that the greatest aspect of my study abroad in Chile was my family. Learning a new language, becoming more independent, seeing more of the world, and learning about a different culture all impacted my life immensely. However, developing these unbreakable relationships with people who were previously strangers was the most rewarding experience of all. Thankfully, technology has made it easier and easier to keep in touch, so we're often in contact over the Internet. I also speak with all of them over the phone during most holidays and birthdays. They always ask when I can come back to visit, and I've been fortunate enough to return multiple times. Each time I visit, I am reminded of how they truly see me...*as a true brother and son.*

—————————

Packing

This is one of the most fun and difficult tasks that you'll have to accomplish before you leave. It can be overwhelming to think about all the things you'll need to take with you. It can also be difficult to decide what goes and what stays in your closet at home.

Here are some things to keep in mind while packing for studying abroad that will make your life much easier:

- **Don't over pack.** You don't need pots and pans. You don't need ten pairs of shoes. You don't need hundreds of shirts. You don't need an entire medicine cabinet. You don't need a library of books! Focus on the essentials like warm clothes, electronics, and any else that's really important to you.

- **Bring some special items.** When you're down or having a bad day, what types of things make you feel better? The reality is - you're going to experience some lonely moments while you're abroad. Maybe for you it's a few pictures from home, your new iPod, or a jar of extra chunky peanut butter! I don't know what it is for you, but having a few of these *small* personal items can help after a couple months away from home.

- **A laptop is necessary.** You're going to need a laptop for everything from schoolwork to keeping in touch with your parents back home. You'll want a few attachments like a headset or microphone as well. You should also install Skype or another program that will let you call home (More information below).

- **Skip the toiletries.** Shampoo, conditioner, deodorant, toothpaste, and other basic toiletries are available around the world. Not to mention the fact that they can be a hassle to get through security, and they take up too much room (and weight) in your luggage.

- **Concentrate on clothes.** Clothes are one of the *main* things that you're going to need, so if you're going to skimp, don't skimp too much on clothes. Laundry will be available, but it can be a real challenge to keep up with it during your weeks of traveling and studying. Remember that you will probably experience two to three seasons during your time abroad, so you'll want to save room for both warm and cold weather (*Check out the average temperature highs and lows for the months of your stay at* www.weatherbase.com)

- **Check your weight.** Okay, not *your* weight, but your suitcase's weight! Places like Wal-Mart and Target sell very cheap luggage scales that allow you to see how much your bag actually weighs. You can also try to put the bag on your bathroom scale at home. Do a "pre-pack" a few days beforehand and compare your luggage's weight to that of your airline's weight restrictions (*It's usually about 50 lbs per bag depending on airline*) If it's overweight, you'd better think more closely about what you're bringing along. The airlines will charge you for overweight bags, and there are much better ways to spend that money! This goes for study trips and weekend excursions you take while you're abroad as well.

Communications

Keeping in touch with family and friends back home has become very easy nowadays. By researching your options, you will find that you can keep in touch for very reasonable prices no matter where you're traveling.

- As I've noted before, Skype has become the dominant mechanism in international communications for current study abroad students. It's a computer program that allows free computer-to-computer calls, and you can also use it to call cell phones and landlines for pennies a minute. Even if you don't have your own computer or connection abroad, local Internet cafes may be equipped with Skype as its popularity has increased dramatically worldwide.
- Cell phones are also important for keeping in touch, but they're more useful for local communications than international calling

due to the cost. Research if you can take your own phone abroad, and what fees may apply. Some domestic providers do not work internationally so it's important to check on this before you leave. It may be cheaper to get a local phone once you are there since most international phones work on a pay-as-you-go plan. If you get a basic phone and basic plan, this should cost less than $100 in most countries.

· Postal systems around the world vary dramatically in quality. While they can be useful for the novelty of sending postcards or packages, international shipping can be very expensive and delivery systems unreliable. Always keep in mind there may be costs to send packages of value. It is better not to plan to make *snail mail* a part of your primary communication plan.

The stage is now set, you have gathered the necessary tools for living and studying abroad. Now, what should you expect? I realize that not knowing what lies ahead can be scary. Unfortunately it's also the very thing that deters most students from ever leaving in the first place. However now that you have all your pre-departure items taken care of, you can relax for a while. Soon you will be submersed in unfamiliar lands not knowing exactly how to act or what to do, so let's switch gears and talk a little about getting acclimated to the local culture.

3. Culture Culture Culture

Let me start this topic by giving you a real life example of what I experienced in Loyola's structured Spring Break trip to North Africa...(sometimes a little organized structure is a good thing!)

Spring Break in Tunisia, North Africa:

To give you an idea of what went down, here is a snapshot of the events we experienced during this

weeklong study trip: Arrival in Tunis, a visit to the town of Sousse, a unique viewing of a presentation and question/answer **session** at the U.S. Embassy of Tunisia, A trip to the city of Gammarth. A trip to Sidi Bou Said- town overlooking the Gulf of Tunis, a stay at the 5 star hotel Phebus with a free lecture from Yale/Tunisian Professor Hamadi Redissi on the topic of "Islam and Democracy in the Arab World" followed by lunch with thirty-five English speaking Tunisian law students (this might have been my favorite part of the whole trip), learning how to barter in the markets with the law students after lunch, A post- lunch lecture from a few of the Professors from the University in Tunis about "Islam and Women". A visit to the Punic war city-state of Carthage, followed by a trip to the United States Military Cemetery where the troops killed in North Africa during World War II were put to rest. An unexpected excursion to the sanctuary of the tophet- the sacrificial site of the Carthaginian Empire, seeing the Punic ports, more lectures in Carthage, visits to the Roman amphitheater in El Jem, a trip to the underground troglodyte dwellings of the Star Wars movies- including the famous "bar scene" in the original Star Wars movie, an overnight trip to the desert oasis town of Douz- bordering the Sahara desert, a camel trek into the Sahara wearing a turban and authentic desert clothing. We rode in 1994

Toyota Land Cruisers to the Habibi campsite, which was about 15 km into the Sahara desert and then camped there overnight in eight-person tents. We took a side trip to Chott el-Jarid sal "lake" which is where parts of the film- *The English Patient* were filmed… another Star Wars ghost town visit to a place called Tatoween which was constructed by Director, George Lucas. A stay at the Hotel Tamerza, which just happened to five-star. Jeep rides through Seldja Gorge and into the canyons to hike in the mountain oasis's known as Chebika and Tamerza. A ride on the famous Red Lizard Train in pursuit of the North African Atlas Mountains capped off the night. Then, seeing the Roman Ruins at Sbeitla and staying in the coastal resort town of Hammamet the following day. A short trip to the holiest city in the Muslim world other than Mecca and Medina -- A place called Kairouan (home of "the great mosque"), A private tour of the Aghlabid Basins, the Sidi Sahbi Mausoleum, and the Medina- all in Kairouan. Well, that… that's about it. But really it's not even close.

My memory was running short and culture shock had set in. Wake up calls, buses, and more buses were always on stand-by, waiting to take us to one of the many exotic destinations in our itinerary. We were always on the move in Tunisia, never time to waste! Every minute, no, every second of this trip was used to the fullest. Before this, I'm not sure Tunisia would have made my "top ten list of places to go for Spring Break." Sometimes you have to be open to the possibilities and let it ride... because it was better than I could have ever imagined.

After all, those events above are simply a list. That was merely a brief outline of **some** of the events we partook in on our spring break study trip in the recently French-occupied country of Tunisia, North Africa. There is a completely distinct feeling you get before, during, and after an adventure like this ~ one that is entirely planned for you before departure.

There I was, holding a schedule. It was a piece of paper outlining the sites we were going to see, places we were going to explore, and the many hotels (and tents) we were going to sleep in. It included everything from the important professors we were going to meet to the freaking canyons we were going to scale, and much more.

The culture in Tunisia was one I hadn't yet become comfortable with, and I could hardly pronounce the names of most of the towns we were scheduled to visit. I was living through an itinerary so specific and comprehensive that even the slightest delay could throw off an entire day's plans. Due to this small margin of error, you may think the spontaneity would be limited on this trip... but not in Tunisia. The experience was priceless. There is no conceivable way I could capture the whole ordeal on paper, but there was one event we had the privilege to experience that taught me a little about the real culture in Tunisia.

We arrived early one afternoon to a nature-lit, marble built dining room full of stone fountains. They were equipped with hidden speakers playing a familiar tune *"Fur Elise"* by Ludwig Van Beethoven. A little on the *"twilight-zone"* side I would say, but still inviting nonetheless. There we were, one hundred young American students ready to share our culture with a group of intelligent, slightly older Tunisian law students... all thirty-five of them. There were no assigned seats, so I decided to do what any twenty-one year old red-blooded American guy would do... look for the 'friendliest' faces.

At a small table right in the center of the room were two of the prettiest, dark-skinned, brown-eyed twenty-five year old Tunisian law students. My roommate

Sean and I acted quickly and snatched a seat next to the young women. I looked around and noticed all the local guys were small and gaunt. Most of them wore neckties or suit jackets, which I was not expecting in North Africa due to my ignorance and pre-developed notions about the culture. Based on these observations, I knew Sean and I probably stood out in the crowd since we are both 6'3" and had on athletic clothes. We sat there, fidgeting, and slightly uncomfortable with our new surroundings.

How could I break the ice? A smile is universal I thought, so I made sure to do it often while trying to come up with some interesting questions. But before I could open my mouth, the attractive young woman next to me asked "wow, what sport do you play" I was so thrown off at first, I just laughed and answered her question with fragile confidence (and slowly so she could understand). However, her English was completely comprehensible. She even mocked me after detecting how slowly I was speaking for her benefit. I was very impressed, and I began to doubt everything I had assumed about the Tunisian culture.

There were still times when we would share a laugh and I would try to help her come up with the right slang words to tell or joke or make a point, but that was all the direction I had to give. After all, I couldn't formulate much more than a few sentences in Arabic or French, but she was fluent in all of them. This was interesting, and the conversation quickly centered on the different aspects of each other's cultures. I wanted to know specifically about the roles of women; because I had to ask why she had peppered my chicken, poured my drink, placed my napkin on my lap, and took care of everything I could possibly need. She explained that in the Muslim world, it is the woman's job at the table to cater to any need the men may have... no matter how simple it might be. Another topic we delved into was the differences we noticed in places like Egypt and Tunisia. We witnessed evidence of widespread poverty, corruption, and strict attitude towards religion and women in Egypt. However these issues were not as apparent in Tunisia. We talked about the problems that exist in an Islamic declared state not separated from government. I learned so much more about a culture I had previously studied in school, and thought I knew so much about. I was wrong about a lot of it, but I was silently giving thanks to the founding fathers of democracy when we talked about politics. Living in a democratized society was a wish our hosts conveyed with passion, and I couldn't argue with that one.

The conversation was endless and intriguing. The four and a half hour lunch went by so quickly -- like we were at a drive-in. But of course, we were in Africa so it must have been the great company. We continued the afternoon exploring the most famous Medina in North Africa while the girls helped us barter with the shop owners. Thanks to our gracious hosts, it was a task I was slowly but surely getting the hang of. We took several pictures, exchanged contact information, and finally parted in a local date and pastry shop at the end of town.

I discovered something that day... not something entirely new, but it was something very true. I thought about how similar we really were to each other, and how I believed something so different about these people only ten hours earlier. I was ill informed, and fairly close-minded about the Tunisian culture and its people. Maintaining ignorance of these fundamental traits in other human beings and their culture erects violence, oppression, apathy for change, and other associated problems. I saw none of these issues on this day, in the heart of an Islamic state... now integrated with US.

This experience in Tunisia undoubtedly changed my view of the world and the nature of Islam. When I was hanging out with the local law students, I truly felt, even if only for a moment, a part of *their* culture.

Learning about other cultures

Now I know when many people think of culture, they think of museums, theatre, and other forms of art. That's Culture with a capital C. You'll definitely encounter some of that while you're studying abroad — probably a *lot* of it if you're going to Europe. But what about culture with a lowercase *c*? I know what you're probably thinking — there is no difference at all! Actually, there are a few distinctions, and I will explain more about the type of culture I experienced in North Africa.

Culture with a small c refers to our social norms — the things we learn growing up about how to function within society. What is the proper way to behave in school or while watching a classical music performance? How do you hold your fork and knife? Do you even *use* a fork and knife for that matter? What is the best way to approach a street full of traffic? How do you handle it when someone compliments you? These are only some of the ways we exemplify different cultures.

There are about a thousand examples of what culture is- from obvious things like what we think is good to eat, to more obscure stuff like how we relate to each other and our ideas about morality. There are hundreds of different cultures around the world, and even though the country you live in does not always define them, nationality definitely plays a part in characterizing one's culture.

What is Culture Shock?

Culture shock happens when you move from one culture that you are very comfortable with to a new culture that forces you to stay on your toes. Culture shock feels a little bit different to each person, but almost everyone experiences some form of culture shock, especially during his or her first experience living abroad.

Understanding what culture shock is and how it can affect you is a crucial step in making your adaptation process run smoothly. If you can pinpoint the phases as they happen, you will be much better equipped to say to yourself, "It's okay I recognize these uncomfortable feelings I know they will pass." Sadly, it isn't uncommon for study abroad students to become completely overwhelmed by all of the differences they're experiencing. Unfortunately for them, the challenge seems too much to handle, and they go home. I know this will not happen to you, though, because you're doing your research. You will have the knowledge and the correct mindset to deal with whatever comes your way, including culture shock.

The W-Curve

Most intercultural scholars agree that culture shock and adaptation to a new environment occur over the course of months. They happen in phases that can more or less be described using a simple graph called the "W Curve."

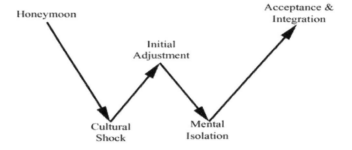

An Example of a W-Curve for Culture Shock Phases

Although everyone experiences cultural adaptation in different ways, you'll probably go through one or more of these phases at some point during your time abroad.

Phase 1: *Honeymoon Phase* – Everyone knows that honeymoons are all about champagne on the beach and romance, and comparatively, that's what your first one to three months in your new country will be like. Everything will seem outrageous, interesting, and downright awesome. Make no mistake: this is no drug-induced euphoria (I hope) you're simply exploring the contrasts and idiosyncrasies of the new culture.

Phase 2: *Culture Shock Phase* – By this time, the honeymoon will be over. Suddenly, you might feel annoyed by all of the little things that you didn't notice at first. Simple things like taking the subway or going to classes might feel like a crisis. This is the most difficult of all the cultural adaptation phases because the feeling of isolation is heightened. You might feel that you're having trouble making friends, or that none of the locals are very friendly. Or you might feel like you're tired of your new environment and wish you were back home. It's critical for you to persevere through this stage, even if the negative emotions become intense.

Phase 3: *Initial Adjustment Phase* – At about three months in, things will start to normalize. Going to the grocery store will no longer seem like an activity that makes you want to take the next flight out of town. You'll start to appreciate things more; you will be more interested in your classes and lectures as well. If you can make it to this phase, you're pretty much home free.

Phase 4: *Acceptance & Integration Phase* – This phase only happens after you've spent over six months in your new environment; therefore, many study abroad students never reach this phase because they only stay for one semester. Once you reach the Integration Phase, you'll feel truly at home in the new culture. A few things might bother you here and there, but generally your new country will feel totally normal—much like home. You've got friends, you can speak the language fluently enough to focus on other things, and you're basically one of the locals.

Phase 5: *Re-entry Phase* – This isn't represented on the graph, but going home is probably one of the hardest things you'll have to do. This might surprise you now, but it isn't something to take lightly. When you return home, you will notice changes within yourself as you look at your home culture through a new set of "international specs." The problem is that your friends and family won't know what you've been through. They might seem apathetic, or just not as excited as you expected. Do not take this personally; it's just one of those things where *you had to be there*. Furthermore, the customs you've adopted in the new country don't apply back home, and you might feel confused and isolated as you are suddenly expected to return to old cultural habits. However as time passes, these things will become familiar again, and home will suddenly feel like, well — *home* again.

Cross-cultural differences can sometimes seem overwhelming—and plentiful enough to fill all the oceans in the world. When living in a new culture, it can feel like you have to do all the adapting that no one around you has to adapt at all. However, that's pretty much the way it works. After arriving in a new culture, you have to expect to do things *their* way. Remember the old adage, "When in Rome ... " Well, it certainly holds true for any type of study abroad experience.

To minimize stress, be sure to research local norms so you are aware of cultural differences. What kinds of clothing will be acceptable? Do you need to remove any type of piercing or accessory? How should you address your professors? What expectations are there for students? It helps to know what the locals expect from you in order to avoid any conflict.

The good news is it's very easy to become aware of the cultural differences you face, and it isn't too hard to overcome them. Some of the most common cultural differences include the following:

- *Communication problems* – We Americans generally like to say everything we mean right up front for the sake of efficiency and to avoid error. However, in other cultures, they sometimes like to leave things open for interpretation. You might find yourself totally confused by what other people mean, even if you're speaking the same language. When you're researching your future home, make sure to investigate communication styles. If possible, meet up with someone on campus from that country and ask them what they found most surprising about American communication. That will give you some hints about what to expect on the other end.

- *Etiquette* – Did your parents ever tell you it was rude to stare? Well that just isn't true in China. In fact, staring is considered a compliment! And you were probably taught not to eat with your hands (except for pizza), but in India, they *only* eat with their hands. And in Russia it's customary to leave a little food on your plate to let the host know there was enough to eat while in other countries it's rude to let food go to waste. Try to have fun breaking American social rules (assuming it's polite in your new country). This might be the only time you can get away with it!

- *Time schedules* - Would you believe it actually is not rude in some places to show up an hour late to meet your friends for dinner? In Ireland, for instance, people are routinely late. If someone tells you they'll see you at eight, you may want to hold off ordering them a Guinness, because it will probably get warm. Feel free to conform for the moment, but don't develop any bad habits just because it's customary for the locals to do it--make sure you represent yourself and your country to the fullest.

- *School expectations* - All of the above can combine in completely crazy ways to affect the expectations at school. Professors might show up late for classes (or students, for that matter), or give little-to-no instruction on how to do a project or assignment. It might be rude to ask questions in class, or rude not to, depending on where you are. Additionally, you might find yourself completely bewildered by what your local classmates are doing on any given task. This is your opportunity to soak up everything and learn all that you can. Step up, and don't be shy to ask questions about anything you don't understand.

    Shopping Tactics ~ Bargaining is a way of life in many places abroad. Practice before you go, and be prepared to haggle for goods in marketplaces. You should research local bargaining traditions, and develop confidence with numbers in the local language. That way, you can always get the best deals during your time away from home.

Overcoming Cultural Shock

If you reach the point where culture shock is winning and you just want to go home, you've got to stop and say "I'm tougher than this. If I quit now, I may regret it for the rest of my life! Goodbye culture shock." It may sound ridiculous to treat the situation this way, but it actually works. How do you do that, you ask? It all starts with your mindset. Just *decide* to step up and understand that you have control over how you react to any and all situations. In other words, you can dictate what "culture shock" really means to you and how it ultimately affects you.

Make sure to put in some preparation work in various cultural areas you are unsure of. This includes learning a bit of the local language and understanding how to fit into the dominant life rhythms.

Strategies

- Studying the language is helpful for cultural integration, and getting around town. You don't have to become an expert before you arrive, but getting through a few lessons will really help. Be able to ask for basic directions, a bathroom, and any other personal 'musts' you have such as the gym or dance club.
- Learn how to read the local menus. Don't put any additional pressure on yourself when it comes to a new culture's food. If there are any foods you cannot tolerate, make sure you learn how to convey your needs properly.
- Use the first few days to explore. You might even want to plan your flights so you arrive a couple days early. This will give you plenty of time to breathe and get acclimated. Take a whiff of the air, get a sense of the city's layout, check out your university's campus, and learn the bus system. These are the basics for getting around, and you don't want to be

scurrying to class the first day without knowing which bus you need to take.

- Meet people. Go to every single social outing you can. I don't care if you suspect the other guests are lougie-hawking communists, just go. Odds are, you'll meet one or two nice people, and get on the road to making local friends which can be priceless.
- Stay in touch with the people back home. This is crucial in the first few days abroad. You might find yourself wandering the wet cobblestone streets of Rome or the crowded, yet lonely Hutongs of Beijing. That's when you might need to talk with someone you love from back home.

Exploring cultural myths and mysteries

What is one of the greatest pleasures of living abroad? Hooking up with the hot Italian bar tender, you say? Maybe. But trust me, learning the myths and mysteries of the culture where you're studying is much more fulfilling. To do this, you're going to need to know what the clichés and stereotypes are in your new culture. Does everyone wear berets and sneer at foreigners in France, or is that just a stereotype? Are all Brazilians beautiful and excel at *futebol?*

One amusing way to do this is to make a list of the things you've heard about in [insert your study abroad country here] and some things you expect might be true about the country before you leave. Think of everything you can, even if you feel it might be a little bit offensive. This will help clear out the "guts" right away. Put the list out of sight in your journal or notebook. You might want to make a note at the top of the page saying "Stereotypes or realities?" Just remember to keep it tucked away so no one finds it and gets the wrong idea.

Bring the list out after you've spent a few weeks or even months abroad. What have you learned about this new culture? Which of your preconceived notions were true? And which were total rubbish?

This type of exercise will help you to figure out *exactly* what to believe about your new culture. It will help you overcome your own prejudices, and keep you from disclosing any false information in the future. Knowing these facts will help you learn the new and wonderful mysteries that abound in your study abroad country.

4. Language Barriers... and so much more

Finding Clarity in Madrid, Spain:

My primary take on Spanish-American relations came while in Tunisia, in the form of a thin, immature, curly haired Spanish guy with intensely crooked teeth. He decided to take a detour while in pursuit of his hotel room and slither his way into ours. Our whole group had just arrived at a new hotel, and barely got a chance to set our bags down when he came in.

I started out puzzled, startled, and just put-off by this person's lack of manners when he entered our room. He immediately started yelling various Spanish phrases relating to his beloved city of Madrid and their notorious soccer team of "Real." Thanks to my entire three semesters of formal Spanish instruction, I could understand most of the things he was saying. He proceeded to try and ask us where we were from and what we were doing in Africa. No one wanted to disclose any information, and were confused... Why did he feel the need to barge in on us and sputter all these words about Madrid? My patience was quickly running short.

This guy already violated our preference for personal space, so it was difficult to remain calm and controlled. Additionally, our sporadic feelings of peace and comfort were already fragile due to the ten-hour bus ride we had just endured. He must have heard me speak English when I told Sean to ask him to leave-

"Hey, go sleep it off bro" Sean told him.

His little dark eyes immediately grew wide, like two black holes about to swallow the Universe. He exclaimed "Odio America, usted no es libre, George Bush es estupido, y somos las unicas democracias!" (He was comparing Spain to the United States... claiming how they have more freedom, along with G.W. remarks, and various racial and profane comments about Barack Obama) I couldn't believe what I was witnessing.

I should also mention that earlier in the day we visited the American World War II cemetery in North Africa. Most of us departed the cemetery with a renewed, and unexplainable level of love and appreciation for our country. This experience only added to the tension in the room.

We had had enough with this clown, but instead of sinking to this man's small-minded level, we said nothing. Instead, we just backed him up till we could shut the door. I was burning inside, but at the same time I wondered why this random person from Spain could change my mood so quickly and cause me to experience all these intense emotions about my own country. Was it the shock factor? The military cemetery? Homesick for my country perhaps? It was probably a combination of all these things... but I also knew I would be in this man's homeland in less than a week.

When you're displaced in a country very far from home, I've found it's helpful to search within yourself and constantly reflect on how you're feeling. I was still somewhat disturbed about this surprising, albeit minor confrontation we just had. But why would it matter so much? Where was this coming from?

No one can avoid being ridiculed at some point in his or her life. You may have been weaker than a bully who was looking to pick a fight; or you could have been different in some way from all the "cool" kids? (I know, imagine that...) You could have been picked last on the kickball team at school, or you were just the butt of every joke and that was that. Sometimes when things would get bad, you'd have to go home and explain it to your parents. The inevitable response from them would come from a place of love, but regardless of the situation, they'd probably tell you it's because those mean kids just want to be like you.

I never really had much faith in the notion that someone would get a kick out of hurting another person just because of jealousy. To me that statement was merely a way to appease the pain I was feeling. I always knew that everything would eventually be okay, and the problem was that some people were just born nasty. However I had been immersed in examples of this on a regular basis since arriving abroad. Just walking through a certain town, I could witness countless examples supporting that jealously is usually the prime fuel of hatred.

Before I left for Spain, I got the opportunity to practice some of my language skills at the corner cafés in Italy and France. The locals and I would invariably discuss each other's homeland and reputation. To my immediate surprise, I heard adjectives such as "materialistic" "boastful" and "excessive" when they tried to describe the way most of *their* citizens view the United States. Upon further investigation, I found out that many groups of locals looked upon westerners as money-hungry, and very desperate for attention.

It was shocking because different demographics conveyed similar attitudes, and I wasn't completely sure why. Was it an over-simplified case of envy? Through all the different types of people I came across, I would receive the same looks and inquisitions about where I'm from. When I told them United States, they would usually tell me how lucky I am, and how they wished they could reside amongst us in America. Some of them even stated that it was their life's dream to make it into the United States one day. As an acute observer in each new surrounding, I heard this time and time again. However many of these people were also quick to criticize, or even express their utter hatred for American citizens and the American way of life. Meanwhile, I thought about the thousands of foreigners who have risked their lives just for a chance to cross the border and establish a new life. Despite all the mixed remarks, I knew for certain the U.S. held something of enormous value.

It became much clearer to me after I thought about our run-in with the obnoxious man from Madrid. America is, in many ways, seen as a fascination... an object of desire for those who bash her most. Of course, there are many who express this view and are perfectly content on where they are, and they truly don't have the slightest desire to change.

It seems that a lot of these problems could be corrected if we all had the ability to effectively communicate. Some people think Americans are unwilling to learn other languages, and that it's the responsibility of the whole world to adapt to us. I learned that it is very beneficial to always try your best to start a greeting or conversation in the local language. I noticed that doing this automatically softens their expressions, opens them up, and always leaves a positive impression. In the same way, my preconceived notions changed just as quickly when they acknowledged my efforts to communicate. Now more than ever, I believe that a perceived effort to adapt, and communicate in any personal encounter is the key to securing a positive experience with foreigners. Accomplishing this one thing could forever change a person's attitude about you and the country you live in. I had to remember this on my next trip to the mysterious lands of Spain...

Off to Madrid! This Central city of Spain served as the perfect platform to brush up on my language skills, see some extraordinary art, and taste some of their famous Sangria. I felt like a real traveler at this point; I was quickly finding myself in very different places each and every week. Of course, this was relative to my "normal" life back home. You know... those months of working, studying for finals, and finally getting the chance to take that vacation with your friends. Studying abroad was definitely a wildly different lifestyle than back home.

We touched down in Madrid, and for some reason, my head felt like a wrecking ball. My voice sounded like a synthesizer and my vision started to blur. I hoped it wasn't anything serious. All I knew was that I could not smell the roasted ham legs on every street corner, I couldn't taste the authentic sangria, I wasn't able to enjoy the tapas, and my internal temperature was climbing steadily with each hour of sleep I was not getting. But I was in Madrid, and I was determined to make the most of each and every moment I had.

With my senses severely dulled, I trudged through the streets each day, and found that Madrid resembled the United States in many ways. I was surrounded. Not by bitter locals and political extremists... but instead, a very familiar scene. There was Starbucks, Kentucky Fried Chicken, Dunkin Donuts, McDonald's, Burger King, *three Chicago Hotdog stands*, and basically every store that would make westerners feel like they were already back home. Everywhere we went we would ask:

"I need a coffee... who wants Starbucks?

"Hey, I'm short on Euros... KFC anyone?"

It was odd that the Spanish stranger, who had clouded all my thinking in Africa just a few weeks earlier, could reside in a place so similar to my home.

Maybe I shouldn't have let one negative experience color my impression of a whole country of very dignified people... hmmm... is that how all this misunderstanding happens all around the world? I don't know, but it was becoming clearer to me.

After indulging in some of our favorite things from back home, my friends and I decided to go searching for the famous Prado museum. We started asking directions in choppy Spanish while wearing our Cleveland Indians and Chicago Cubs hats. This left the locals with the obvious realization that they were talking to Americans who only spoke *English*. However, it seemed that the Spaniards just wanted to accommodate us. The people we communicated with were eager to do anything they could to meet our needs. Spain became the quintessential location to test our communication skills and observe how the locals would receive us. Having a decent understanding of the local language proved to be useful, and almost every Spaniard we came across wanted to go *out of their way* to help us.

The rest of the weekend in Madrid was spent conversing with locals and seeking out some of the most revered works of art in Europe. The best, in my opinion, was "The Guernica" by Pablo Picasso. It's a controversial painting depicting Picasso's unique perspective on the test-bombs set off in Spain and other parts of Europe by the Nazis during World War II. I stood there gazing at the piece for ninety minutes, no less. The massive black and white scene left us all with an admiring, yet different opinion in the end. We all remained silent, and benefitted from my friend Jim's love of Spanish history as he provided insightful commentary throughout the tour.

In the end, communicating with locals in the enormous parks became one of the most rewarding moments we experienced during the entire semester. It was remarkable how quickly we could pick up the language when we were immersed in the culture. We traversed through the prostitute-littered streets, we ate at several restaurants with cured ham legs dangling in the windows, and attended a Real Madrid game with some friendly Spaniards we met. All these unique events teamed up for an unforgettable, educational, and an eye-opening journey in the heart of Spain.

Make the effort

There's nothing that will discount your good intentions and charm faster than obstacles in communication. Even if you weren't very kind or full of charisma, putting in the extra effort to speak the local language could make all the difference. Believe me, your requests and concerns are much more likely to be fulfilled if you start conversations in the right tongue.

I'm guessing you chose your study abroad country because you knew at least *some* of the local language. If not, that's okay because you will probably learn a lot from just being immersed in the culture. Of course, formal study at your home university is going to be a huge help when you arrive. Although you'll soon discover that no classroom can fully prepare you for communicating with locals. This is partly because learning a language in school is generally grammar-focused, rather than conversational.

Another problem is the lack of slang-speech in textbook instruction, which can be confusing while trying to relate to people on the street. Textbooks usually don't take into account local dialects, accents, and many popular phrases. For instance, if you've been learning French at home, you've probably unwittingly been learning *Parisian* French. However a large number of students studying in France actually end up in the southern part of the country, where the local language is fairly different.

Perhaps you're part of this adventurous group: studying in a country where the locals already speak your language. It would be wrong to say that it isn't easier to study in a country where you don't have to learn the language, because it is. However, if you think you have no language problems to worry about, think again.

Let's take a few examples. You've just moved in to your new apartment in Galway and your roommate asks you to get something for them out of the *press*. Would you immediately go to the **kitchen cabinet**? Or perhaps you're asking for directions to a certain street on your first week in Sydney, and the local shopkeeper tells you to walk up the *pavement* a few doors down. Would you end up in the middle of the road, rather than on the **sidewalk**?

Why is learning the local language important?

Quite simply, language is a key component in maximizing your experience. First of all, it will help you with everyday tasks, such as the ones described above. But more importantly, having even a small understanding of the local language is like knowing the passwords that get you through the doors, and into the entire culture. Simply knowing the ways in which people express themselves can reveal so many cultural nuances, tricks, and tips. Is the language more poetic, like Italian, or more utilitarian, like German? Knowing these types of details give you insight into the local culture - a way to understand that, *Hey, the Italians know how to carry on a good conversation.* Or *Wow, the Germans are very efficient.*

Perhaps these examples seem obvious even without knowing the language, but there are a thousand small nuances that you will only discover through speaking like the natives.

How to pick up the local language

There is no guaranteed way to learn the local language quickly without lots of practice. However, there are a few tactics and suggestions I have to help speed you up a little bit. For instance, you can:

- Carry your phrasebook or a dictionary at all times. Look up words as you need them. Using language in situational context is the best way to memorize it.
- Carry a small notebook and jot down new phrases, slang words, and other tid bits as you learn them. Names for food, your personal interests, and even curse words can enhance your overall skills. Anything that you find

interesting or useful is fair game, and a great way to learn.

- Talk to strangers. Taxi drivers are great for practicing a few useful phrases, such as directions and general inquiries. These types of conversations are a great way to get an idea about how the culture handles small talk.

- Have a beer. Okay, I am not talking about getting totally wasted because, quite frankly, it reflects poorly on everyone and everything you represent. However, enjoying one or two drinks socially can help loosen your fears about messing up, and let you begin talking and practicing while you make a friend or two.

- Don't be afraid of making mistakes. Easier said than done, right? I know, but when you're abroad, being laughed at just doesn't matter that much. If you need to start learning how to laugh at yourself, this can be a great start. But think of it this way: remember that French study abroad student from your chemistry class last semester? Did you even *notice* when he or she made a few mistakes speaking English? No way! All you cared about was that smooth, exotic French accent, and I bet that's what your counterparts think about you speaking their language. Just try your best and have fun with it.

Great activities for language practice

- Take a taxi.
- Chat with a shopkeeper or restaurant server.
- Start slow- ask for the time, bathroom, bank, etc.
- Get involved in a language exchange.
- Find a local study partner.
- Live or hang out with locals.
- Chat with other study abroad students in the local language.
- Host a party.
- Ask for directions, even if you don't need them.
- Ask what things are in a supermarket or shop.
- Ask what things cost in a supermarket or shop.
- Go on a local day trip to practice travel-related phrases.
- Read some local-language books.
- Set your mobile phone to the local language.
- Set your computer to the local language.
- Listen to local music.
- Go to a concert or play.

- Read the newspaper everyday.
- Learn a useful word or phrase everyday.
- Try having a conversation over a beer.
- Take a hobby class such as dance, pottery, or photography...in the local language.
- Have a romance. Yeah, this is perhaps the best motivator to learning a language!

After years of studying in your formal classes, you'll probably discover that spending only a few hours amongst the native speakers was just as educational. However, becoming acclimated to the local language is completely up to you. Think of it as an investment in yourself. If you have the discipline to do it, you will truly maximize your experience. Additionally, understand that putting in the extra effort may come back and save you in the future!

5. Exotic Cuisine or... "What is THAT?"

My Mask of Pleasure in Guilin, China:

Sean and I had decided to take our newly obtained travel knowledge and delve into China for a month to study the culture, and of course, the food. Venturing into the eccentric realms of China and the Far East don't come without some level of

skepticism and apprehension for most
foreigners. Our flight to Beijing would start things
off for us with subsequent stops in cities like Xi'an,
Hangzhou, Guilin, Shanghai, Macau, and eventually
the great city of Hong Kong.

Of all the topics I discussed with family and friends
before leaving for China, the one that always
provoked the most animated conversations was the
food. I had never been to China before, I couldn't
speak Mandarin, and I didn't know a whole lot
about the Chinese culture in general. After years of
seeking out every available American and European
history class I could take to fulfill my course
requirements, I was left with a sparse and somewhat
pathetic understanding of Chinese culture.
Therefore, I decided to stop in the public library and
see what I could do to fill this gap. One book I
discovered was *Lost in Planet China* by Maarten
Troost. The memoir was very entertaining, and the
take-home message I extracted after reading it was
this: Never make assumptions when ordering at a
restaurant in China. Not the most scholarly lesson,
but it definitely made me think. This was hammered
in my brain when I read that he accidentally ordered
sheep's stomach at a restaurant in Beijing. I would
consider myself to be pretty adventurous when it
comes to trying new foods, but just in case I ordered

the innards of a cat, or something, I'd surely like to know about it.

In China, we quickly discovered that when preparing the animal proteins of any dish, nothing is thrown out. Every part of the creature is utilized and consumed. A vegetarian's worst nightmare would become our reality at some point on our trip, I thought. Our first experience with the local cuisine came in Guilin. Even though we were in a massive hurry during this trip, we decided to ditch our protein shakes and try some local meat despite any bad rumors we heard.

As a species, we humans are omnivores, which means we can eat foods that are plant or animal based. However on this day in China, our propensity for consuming meat was dominating, and we were now susceptible to anything prepared for us that night. During the day, however, we had some business to take care of.

We awoke the morning of May 23rd at 5AM in Guilin, China ready to experience the Lee River Cruise, and explore the tourist friendly town of Yangzhou. We arrived the previous night very late, and didn't check in to our hostel until well after 2 AM. With only a few hours of sleep behind us, we inhaled our "American Breakfast" which consisted of a fried egg, white bread, and black coffee. I thought the breakfast was sufficient, but we had not traveled halfway around the world for an egg- on-white bread *express meal.* Up until this point, it seemed like we were always in such a hurry to reach our next destination, that food just became an afterthought. We had already been in China for eight days and we hadn't *really* gone out and sampled the local fare. So we decide to slow down, and try some local food on this night no matter what.

"We need to hit up some authentic Chinese places tonight, man ... this is OK, but I'm tired of all this familiarity" I said to Sean.

"Yeah, we will just relax and finally get some authentic stuff at that place up there when we get home later" he replied, pointing to the enormous top-floor restaurant across the street above the shopping mall.

"I'm good with that, at least we have our Optimum Nutrition protein powder with us in the meantime." I said, "You know, just in case..."

He agreed, and having a protein shake with a handful of nuts was definitely not the worst thing in the world. However we were not going to let our desire for constant efficiency distract us any longer. With that in mind, we decided to take our time and explore Yangzhou, and make the most of our day on the Li River. The view on the river was like a scene from *Jurassic Park*. Endless mountains engulfed with greenery split through the thick, heavy fog that hovered above. This endless gray mist partially impaired our vision of the peaks, but we could tell this was a place to be highly revered and appreciated. I stood out at the edge of the boat and acted like I was George H.W. Bush in a famous photo I had seen of him in the exact place I was standing. It seemed crazy to think that all this was possible. We were in the land of China on this very river that many world leaders had experienced on their visits, and we were doing it all for less money than a Morton's steak dinner in Chicago would cost. (See chapter 6 for more on finances).

We departed from Yangzhou content with our bags of souvenirs, and newfound amazement for the humble little town. In the middle of China, just off the Li River, this quaint village resembles some of the most famous fishing villages in Europe with its tightly packed homes, ethnic restaurants, and endless European style cafés. There were miniature bridges engulfed with moss as narrow creeks flowed endlessly below. It was truly a sight to behold. Retail signs in Chinese characters displaying every color in existence overflowed the busy streets as shopkeepers competed for our attention. Sean was being followed closely by a little Chinese man begging, just for a glance, at his collection of chopsticks and clay pots. His insistence paid off however; as we both forked over twenty-five Yuan to the persistent salesman for a cool souvenir. I found myself strangely disheartened; knowing that the sum of money we spent wouldn't even be enough to buy him a cup of coffee if he wanted. So we bought a couple more, which made his day.

The cruise back was much of the same, and our appreciation for the magnificent scenery before us was stronger than ever. We stood completely silent for the rest of our trip, yet when we returned home we found out we had both been thinking the same thing: when am I going to wake up? The Li River was like living in a dream.

Before we knew it, we were back on a bus en route to our hostel for the night. We decided the first order of business would be to finally go up to that restaurant. It had been a long, yet awe-inspiring trip. But it was time to check out the most notorious, ancient, and misunderstood cuisine in the world... all we had to do is get up and walk out our front door. We jetted through traffic like an enormous Panda Bear of Xi'an was chasing us, until we made our way up to the pristine setting that would be our first real meal in China.

Dozens of eyes from other customers were fixed on us the moment we entered the large room ... but we had come to expect this in China. The waitress let us know right away she did not speak English, which was also no surprise to us. I pulled out my handwritten list of translations I compiled a few months ago that I hoped would be useful. Luckily, I made sure to include a small subsection on basic food and restaurant words. Before we knew it, the entire restaurant staff was hovering over us with wide smiles, ready to fulfill any wish or demand we gave them.

I immediately noticed a picture on the menu of a succulent looking, golden-brown chicken breast "I will have the *Ji*" I said eagerly.

"Ah, Xièxiè (pronounced sheh sheh, 'thank you')" the waitress replied, still smiling.

We also ordered three different vegetable courses at the recommendation of our waitress. Our choices were bok Choy, broccoli, and green beans cooked in bacon fat. This trio of local produce came out from the kitchen in no time as we witnessed the head waitress coming toward our table with two large steaming bowls. Following her were at least seven other waiters eagerly anticipating what the strange foreigners' reaction would be.

Each vegetable course was presented in a large family style dish as one of the staff members directed Sean and I on the proper way to set up our plates. The first two dishes of bok Choy and broccoli exuded prominent flavors of garlic and soy sauce, and then finished with a subtler note of sesame. An incredibly satisfying follow up came in the form of semi-greasy green beans lightly sautéed in sesame oil and bacon. At this point, I found myself wondering how I had lived so long without knowing how delicious real Chinese food was, and why anyone would muster a negative word about it. And then I remembered my grandparents telling me that the vegetables they had had in China were by far the best part of their culinary experience. Interestingly enough, I didn't recall many stories about them enjoying any succulent, golden-brown *Ji* in the Far East.

In the heart of Guilin, we sat there content with the offerings, and constant hospitality of the restaurant staff. We were clearly purple elephants in the room amongst the locals, so we couldn't help operating under some level of self-consciousness. After they cleared our plates, we gave our compliments and didn't have to worry about putting up a façade for anyone.

That was until the supposed *Ji* finally arrived at our table. Sean looked as confused as I was upon examining the mysterious dish before us. I looked down and noticed the bleach-white meat still covered with its thick purple veins protruding under a thin film of yellow, poorly plucked skin.

"I think they brought us the wrong food," I said with uncertainty and hope.

Sean agreed, and motioned at the plate with a disapproving, yet polite wave ... the head waitress, looked down with wide eyes and nodded "No, No... Shickun... is OK?"

No mistake. I was dumfounded, and I soon realized that the warnings I received prior to our trip might have been true. I glanced up and scanned the room while noticing at least twenty other tables of Chinese guests still looking at us, still smiling. The whole place was undoubtedly interested in what we would think of their local *Ji*. I picked up my chopsticks with caution, fumbled through some type of organ ... *probably the liver*, and proceeded to taste this mysterious chunk of flesh. The taste sensation was comparable to nothing I've ever had before. My mask of pleasure and contentment must have given way to a more candid expression of disgust. I immediately checked myself, though, and smiled up at our gracious servers ... still chewing the cold, yellow, half-plucked rubber bolus of skin and tissue. I looked around and gave a small wave of respect to our fellow diners while simultaneously wondering how I was going to swallow. I quickly grabbed my warm tea and forced it down like a large pill. I repeated this process at least three more times until I finally had to stop due to that reflex that comes when your stomach is rebelling. Mine had been fighting furiously.

Sean just sat there calmly and ordered some beef that was not only edible, but also fairly appetizing. We doubled up on this relatively palatable red meat as I had the *Ji* wrapped up "for later".

Sean revealed to me that in China, it's customary to blatantly spit out your food at a restaurant if you don't like it. However this was something I simply could not force myself to do no matter how "normal" it would be. It was apparent how proud of their cuisine these people were, and just like in any culture I've been to, food is not only a source of nourishment... it's a potent representation of one's cultural identity. So the *Ji* may have been an acquired taste? or I had a young chef make a couple rookie mistakes in cleaning it? Whatever the case, it seems like the Chinese have an unbelievable level of respect for whatever goes under the knife, in the pot, and eventually on our plates.

Given the history of China's unique social infrastructure, it isn't surprising to know that when preparing my chicken, everything was used and nothing was thrown out. You don't travel to far-away lands for the certainty and comfort of it all, you go to try things like *Ji* and have the locals stare at you while wondering what the hell you're going to do. I know now that I will always project gratitude and appreciation for one's culture out of respect, but in reality, it might only be my proverbial mask... hiding my discomfort.

There are many uncertain moments you'll have while studying abroad. One of the most trying will be when you are seated around a table with strangers in a foreign land. What will you do when you're presented with a plate of food that is completely unrecognizable to you? Pick at it? Shove it around? Quickly try a taste to see what it's like? Serve it to the nearby houseplant!?

Food can be an extremely delicate subject, and certain cultures may treat food very differently than you might expect. No matter where you study abroad, there is going to be a moment when you are offered something that looks and seems very unappetizing to you.

How you handle these situations depends on a variety of factors. You're not going to want to offend your hosts. If hosts are serving you, this often means that you should at least try a bite of whatever it is no matter what. Unless you have an allergy, it's worth it to step out of your comfort zone in these situations. If every fiber in your body is rebelling at the thought of taking a bite, then try to claim allergies against some ingredient. However you'll have to know exactly what you're being presented with, and sometimes asking "*what is this?*" just isn't an option.

If you go this route that's all right, but you will probably regret it later on.

Part of the *Truth* is: food is going to play an enormous role in the discovery of your study abroad culture. Learning about what the locals eat, how they eat, and what their relationship to certain foods are can really teach you a lot about the people in general. Try to embrace their culinary habits and traditions no matter what...you may never get another chance again.

Opening one's mind and palate to different foods

The first step is to open up and get curious about experiencing a new culture's cuisine. This will likely be a self-motivated endeavor, but there are many ways to help you get going. Watching shows like *No Reservations* or *Bizarre Foods* on the Travel Channel or www.YouTube.com can help spark your interest. I would often try to satisfy my hunger in the most convenient and efficient way possible. However, instead of submitting to the protein bar in my backpack, I would try and think of an episode I saw, or book I read about discovering a new culture's food. I'd then think about where I was, and the possibilities that existed all around me. I'd get incredibly curious, and forget all about doing what was "convenient." The fact of the matter is that most of the time; you *aren't* going to be presented with anything nasty to eat. The food will be different, but it's usually something delicious that you'll crave when you get back home.

One great strategy is trying to eat everything once, and rule out certain items later. In some cases, however, this might not be an option for you. Perhaps you are vegetarian, you have an allergy, or maybe you just can't stomach the thought of eating an insect. That is okay. Most people around the world are going to understand your troubles with unfamiliar food. Most likely, they'll just laugh at you for squirming in the presence of such a *delicious treat*. Whatever the case, remember that it *is* okay to refuse something just as long as you do it respectfully.

Whatever you do, be gracious. Understand that different people have other ideas about what tastes good, and sometimes these ideas are formulated through hundreds of years of tradition. Respect what other people eat, and politely decline if you absolutely have to.

Food insights... tell me more!
It's not just about *what* people eat, but also *how* they eat. You might notice that in comparison to the way

you eat at home, people in your study abroad country spend a much longer time over meals, or that they make a huge effort to eat every meal at the table with their families. You might notice that *no one* cooks at home, and everyone eats out at restaurants. You may come to find people eat dinner later, or much earlier than you're used to. Perhaps the locals rush through their meals, or maybe they see that lovable pet of yours as just an excellent choice for dinner! Whatever the case may be, you must be willing to adapt in any situation. Show appreciation, and make the most of your limited time to implement the culinary traditions of your study abroad country.

Learning to eat locally

When you first arrive in your new city, you might feel overwhelmed about the unfamiliar faces, language (s), and laws you have to learn. However you can relax because you have a lot to look forward to when it comes to trying the local food. It may take some extra effort, but I can assure you it will be worth it. When everything feels like a lot of *work* to adapt to a new way of life, the temptation is to say, "Screw it" and head for the Golden Arches. That's okay once or twice per semester, or in those sad moments when the street vendors run out of your favorite Nutella crepes and lamb kabobs. However, you must try to eat locally as much as you possibly can.

Doing this can feel challenging at first, but if you take it slowly, one day at a time, it will eventually get easier. To begin, use the following list to make a game out of discovering the local eating habits. These are just a few of the ways you should explore the local eating habits in your study abroad country:

- ❑ What time do locals eat? Are meals taken earlier or later than you're used to?
- ❑ In general, do people eat out or eat at home for most meals?
- ❑ Is fast food typical?
- ❑ Is food generally expensive or cheap?
- ❑ What kinds of foods will cost you extra?
- ❑ Is there a staple food - something served at most meals?
- ❑ Is there a lively street food culture?
- ❑ Where do most locals shop for groceries - in a supermarket, farmer's market, butcher shop, some kind of specialty store, etc?
- ❑ How can you classify the local cuisine? Spicy and hot? Lots of dairy? Meat and potatoes?
- ❑ What kinds of portions do locals typically eat?

- ☐ What kinds of foods are taboo? *Why* are they taboo?
- ☐ What types of eating utensils (if any) are used regularly in this country?

After you've spent a week or two exploring and answering the above questions, you should ask yourself this: **Is there anything about the food and eating habits in this culture that is uncomfortable or distasteful to me?** When you answer this question, spend some time thinking about why the answer(s) you came up with are distasteful or uncomfortable, and see if you can't begin to eradicate those beliefs so you can make the most of it all. The more time you spend thinking about the food, stepping outside your comfort zone, and trying new things, the more content you'll be with your entire food-related experience.

Now, if you're one of those people who might be thinking, *what is the point? I can just eat at McDonald's in any country!* To that, I would say: **Why are you studying abroad in the first place?** If you aren't prepared to take any risks, and that includes culinary risks, then you ought to just pack your bags and go home. I know you won't do that, though. If you are the kind of person who has decided to study abroad-you're probably ready to discover all sorts of new challenges others wouldn't even think about.

Strategies for cooking

Studying abroad will teach you many new life skills and lessons about yourself; learning the local cooking techniques is no exception. How apt you'll be at cooking abroad depends on your motivation to learn, rather than your skills. However if you have a knack for the culinary arts already, then it will just be less hassle while you're abroad.

One thing you'll notice when you try cooking in a foreign country is the low cost of quality, fresh ingredients. Don't expect to find an abundance of microwave dinners and frozen veggies, because in most places they're just not available. This slight lack of convenience can take some time getting used to. Although, after a few weeks you'll likely forget all about your pre-packaged delights, and start to really appreciate this old world approach to meal preparation.

The first step is to go back to your list from above — Where do most locals shop for groceries? The best way to figure this out is to find a local friend to offer some advice on the nearest markets. The next best way is to get online and start searching in your area, and the third way is to take it upon yourself to explore the city until you find a decent store or market. Just don't forget your map! And here is a tip: in most parts of the world, especially Europe, you are expected to bring your own grocery bags. You could even be charged for taking plastic bags, so invest in a backpack or a few reusable cloth grocery sacks for shopping trips.

The next step is to learn what the basic ingredients, spices, and cooking supplies are in your area. In Japan, that might be rice, seaweed, and soy sauce. In India, simple curry spices are obligatory ... and in Germany, you'd better have potatoes on hand. Whatever the ingredients are, be sure to have at least a few of these simple things in your kitchen at all times. This is one of the best parts...stocking up at the markets before you begin cooking.

You may want to start out by trying a local recipe. Why not invite a local food-savvy friend to show you how to cook? You might surprise yourself when you obtain guidance like this. Even in a student household, it is not uncommon to make pasta from scratch in Italy, or fresh stir-fries in China. It's just a way of life, and you will reap the benefits if you ask a friend to help. A perfect way to arrange this is to ask some local friends to do a language and food exchange party. This way you can all get together and practice your speaking skills and learn to cook the traditional dishes of your host country.

If your first meal adheres to your region's standards for tradition, quality, and excellence, then you need to start teaching your friends because that's a gift. However, don't get discouraged if your meal falls flat. Pick yourself up and try again after asking your roommates for suggestions on how you can improve. Sample a different recipe or work on perfecting the one you have. The goal is to stay away from the local fast food joints for as long as you possibly can. If you stay the course, your perseverance in this area will pay off down the line. Learning to cook with local ingredients is a priceless skill you'll have for the rest of your life if you develop it now as a student.

Finally, after you find success with the traditional fare, you might want to try making a few recipes from home just to add some variety. Obviously this is going to depend significantly on what types of ingredients are available. One easy thing you can make with just a few basic ingredients is barbecue sauce, and you'll probably be able to find some type of chicken to go with it. Corn on the cob is also fairly common in markets, and as street food around the world. Lastly, you won't have any trouble finding tomatoes and noodles to make spaghetti no matter where you are. The key to all this is to learn, develop confidence, share with friends, have fun, and enjoy eating.

6. Financial Planning

Conforming to Luxury in Paris, France:

This particular trip to the heart of France left us a little uneasy because we had so much we wanted to accomplish. Some of us were running short on Euros, however, and we knew that Paris was not the best place to be scraping for change. Our aspirations and goals for this trip seemed to be far away because of the short time we had to accomplish everything we wanted.

A concrete, and cost-effective plan to go about it all never made it to our "To Do Lists" before leaving. Therefore, Sean and I decided to suck it up and sacrifice a little... okay... *some* more cash to make the most of our time in Paris. This was not a comfortable alternative by any means, but I realized that in the grand scheme of things the money would not matter. Twenty years from now, I knew that I would only remember the authentic events and five-star dinners we would enjoy. We already had a reservation at one of the most highly acclaimed cafés in Paris, so there was no turning back now. All in all I knew that I would not miss the extra couple hundred Euros, but I would most certainly regret sidestepping through Paris, France while searching for the nearest discounted baguette stands.

We arrived in Paris around 2 o'clock in the morning... just in time to check into our hostel. We opted to choose one of the more reasonably priced lodges for this particular trip. That's why I wasn't surprised when I saw nothing more than a couple of rickety, non-finished wooden staircases leading to a handful of shady entryways. However, this place was looking like it was going to be torn down. Before I could pick up my bags and head to the nearest 4 Euro a night bunk shack, Sean stopped me. He told me that this was just a culture thing in France. The French place more of an emphasis on keeping the inside of a particular building nicely kept, and it matters *much* less what the outside looks like. After quickly checking in, we decided to head out and see what we could find.

The subway system in France is extremely conducive to foreigners, and probably the best forms of public transportation I've ever been in, ever. The ticket prices were very reasonable, and we were able to get virtually anywhere we wanted in a matter of minutes. Our entire group was wide-eyed and ready to extract every ounce of French culture we could contain, despite sleeping less than three hours the night before. The first day's festivities kicked off with an excursion to the famous Cathedral of Notre Dame, where the tickets ended up costing us nothing. I couldn't believe a place as beautiful and venerable as the Notre Dame cathedral was free...

"Maybe this wouldn't be such an expensive trip after all," I heard one of our friends say to Sean.

Sean grinned and said, "Touché mon ami. But just in case you're interested... Connor and I researched and made reservations at a restaurant that overlooks the Eiffel tower."

"We are strapped for cash, but we were thinking of going to a club tonight that has free drinks... you guys want in?!" our friend asked.

"Are you sure man? I think it will be a great opportunity to really experience the beauty of Paris." Sean replied.

I could see that our group was not having it. We were all enjoying this ancient and wondrous cathedral together, but it was looking like our group would be parting ways during the night.

I interjected, "I don't plan on coming back to Paris for a while... I say we all go out and take advantage of this short time we have in one of the greatest cities in the world. You won't even care about spending a little extra money a few years from now"

"We don't mind going out to eat at a place close by our hostel and then head to this club. Let's all explore Paris in our own ways and we can share our stories back in Rome," someone said.

"Okay, well let's just see how we all feel" I replied.

When we walked through the cathedral, we could immediately tell how special this place was. The stained glass windows provided an exquisite backdrop for the imposing limestone statues that lined the walkways. This remarkable stained glass was one of the most impressive features of the cathedral, and it really stood out because many Romans didn't use a lot of it. We waited in line together and made our way up the countless concrete stairs that lead to the top of the cathedral. Upon reaching the crest, I noticed many ghastly gargoyles peering out ... watching the city buzzing a few hundred feet below.

We took notes for later reflection, as well as several pictures before making our way back down. We remained silent, and tried to absorb all we were witnessing at this astonishing site. The narrow, twisting staircase was never-ending. It was like a confined path of heavy, thick, weathered concrete that held no alternative escape. I remembered thinking... 40 percent of America probably couldn't even fit through these corridors. If someone were even slightly obese, they'd have to forget about scaling these ancient steps and sharing a view with the gargoyles. However the Eiffel Tower is only a couple metro stops away, so don't fret, America.

As soon as we reached the bottom, our group decided to split up, exchange phone numbers, and go our separate ways. We were all content, and perfectly willing to respect each other's wishes in Paris. Every weekend trip abroad is a very fluid situation. We found out early on that you have to be willing to adapt and conform to each evolving circumstance; otherwise your time can be stressful, and that will dramatically hinder your experience.

Sean and I were set on dishing out a little extra dough to "do Paris right" according to us (*haha*). After seeking out various relics in some of the notorious museums and cathedrals in all of Europe, we found ourselves running down Le Boulevard Saint-Germaine during rush hour. We were in pursuit of a few Cuban cigars to cap off an evening at the famous restaurant, *Cafe de L'Homme*.

After turning down no less than five street vendors who could only offer us black, dried-up imitations, we finally found what we needed at a hole-in-the-wall Tabbachi somewhere next to *L'Arc De Triomphe*. Of course, neither one of us would have really known the difference in quality anyway. The reality is we've probably only smoked two whole stogies between the two of us since turning eighteen, but we were going to pretend to be connoisseurs tonight.

It was already almost 8 o'clock, so we flagged down the first taxi we saw. Sean greeted the driver and used his seven-year French education with perfection to get us exactly where we needed to be. Sean and the cab driver had animated conversations in French the entire way. Their discussion must have been good because the driver gave us a discount on the fare along with some recommendations for where to go tomorrow night. A nice gesture, but we weren't too comfortable with taking any detours to this shady rave bar he was so up on.

"What did you say to him?" I asked

"Nothing... just talked about ... how much we're enjoying Paris... ha-ha, we saved some money, right?" Sean replied

Ambiguity is not the best way to go with me, but I was going to let this one slide since we got an almost-free ride across town. We gazed up at the flickering white lights that read "afé de hom" as certain letters were burnt out in the sign. This wasn't too promising, but then we entered through two twenty-foot doors and remembered that in Paris, it's the interior that counts. We stumbled upon a hostess wearing a beautifully crooked and seductive smile. When we told her our names she looked down at her clipboard, looked back up at us, and gave us a wink...

In a smooth French accent, she said to us, "come with me, I show you our best table for view"

She led us toward the back of the vibrant, yet dimly lit dining room where a single-file line of waiters stood... in preparation to disclose all of what Cafe de L'Homme offered. We took a seat, in awe of our surroundings because the setting seemed only fit for kings. Walls were replaced by windows, and anytime we looked up, we could watch the Eiffel tower as it sparkled against the pitch-black night sky.

Our waiter sauntered over and presented us with the house specials, along with a complimentary glass of champagne. It was an unexpected gesture that would only have us asking for a whole bottle to split. His casual recommendations of salmon tartare, Le Steak Maison, and waffles with Nutella for dessert were tremendous additions to a truly unforgettable experience.

The Eiffel Tower would explode with beaming bright sparkles every thirty minutes during the night. The time was going by so fast that it seemed like the tower sparkled every five minutes. We sat comfortably at the "best table for view" until 2 o'clock in the morning as the once-full dining room slowly changed. The tables were empty, along with the bottle of champagne, and we were left with our gracious hosts still eager to provide us with their services.

We talked all night about the various times in our life when taking risks paid off, and how making the choice to study abroad seemed like an exciting risk at the time. We both spoke about how we couldn't imagine going through college without taking this opportunity to see the world, and see first hand how *other* people lived. It was a lesson that could not be taught in any classroom or lecture hall. We were given immense freedom from our home institutions to make some discoveries, and it was paying off big time.

We came to a point in the night when we realized that our trip in Paris was worth every penny we spent. And when the check came, we thought we were robbing them! Often times it literally pays to be tight with your cash, especially as a student. But it's also crucial to decide when to make a sacrifice. In the very end ... what will you really care about? The unique experiences I've had with friends in times like this will always win out over things like going out to drink and party. Our time in Paris was done *the right way* according to us; find the best way for you, and it will be a trip you'll remember forever.

We had decided ahead of time that Paris would be a good place to spend some money on the finer things in life. In order to afford the high-class meals, Cuban cigars, decent champagne, and gifts for friends, some other luxuries had to be sacrificed. Cheap hostels once again saved the day for us. You're not going to be spending much time in your room, so look for least shady, yet cheapest place to stay. Doing this will make up for all the important expenditures like food, souvenirs, and other unique opportunities in the city.

With that being said, I think it's fair to say that of all the things that you have to take care of before and during your study abroad stint, money is the most salient element. Most study abroad students dread dealing with the ever tricky money situation ~This includes all of the paperwork and financial arrangements you will need to get in order. Paying for tuition, finding scholarships or grants, budgeting, exchanging money, dealing with currency exchange rates, and finding a job are all part of studying abroad.

If you take the time to budget and handle your finances correctly, you can come away with a lifetime of sound financial habits... and an intimate knowledge of international economics. You'll learn how money works on a global scale, which can be advantageous when applying for future jobs. Another part of the *Truth* is that handling money abroad is no more complicated than handling it at home ~ in fact; you may find that it is actually *easier* to stick to a budget abroad, and not to mention keep out of debt.

Before you go checklist

There are a few things you'll need to take care of at home before you embark on your study abroad journey. Start saving early (about six months early, if possible) and allow yourself a couple of weeks to sort out banking and credit card matters before you leave. Here is a checklist of what you need to take care of financially:

- ❑ Research the local currency norms, as well as the methods for ensuring a smooth financial life while you are abroad.
- ❑ Make sure you have a checking account open with connected ATM and/or debit cards available to draw on.
- ❑ Research your bank fees and credit card charges to be sure you understand the least expensive ways to access cash sources during your stay.
- ❑ Contact your bank to let them know about your travel plans. Make sure they remove any international travel restrictions from your credit and ATM cards.
- ❑ Make sure you have a working pin number with your ATM card and savings account.
- ❑ Make sure all of your credit and ATM cards have an international access symbol, such as

Maestro or Plus. If you're unsure, ask your bank.

❑ Set up your online banking profile and make sure it's accessible from the web.

❑ Be sure that you are able to pay any bills (like credit cards, car insurance, travel insurance) online before you leave. If not, set up automatic debit plans or cancel the services before you leave.

❑ If possible, set up paperless statements for your cards and accounts.

❑ Check with your university's financial aid department about whether your current scholarships, grants or loans will cover your tuition abroad.

❑ Double check that your abroad tuition and fees are paid, either through your university's accounting department or by yourself.

❑ Read up on the exchange rate between your home currency and the foreign country you're heading to.

❑ Learn about the currency of your destination, including denominations and equivalencies. Be aware that many countries are less connected to credit card use than the United States.

How to make a study abroad budget

The first stop on your study abroad budget-making quest is the website or literature from your study abroad university (or your home university's study abroad office). Usually, international offices put together a checklist of estimated monthly budgetary requirements for study abroad students. This should be your place to start for figuring out your monthly budget.

You'll want to take into account:
- Tuition & fees (if they aren't already paid)
- Monthly rent or housing fees
- Food costs
- Transportation costs (most places offer discount public transit cards to students)
- Entertainment costs (how often do you like to go to the clubs, movies, etc.)
- Incidental travel (you'll want to budget in a good amount of money for this so you don't feel guilty taking those weekend trips to other far-off lands... even though they will be totally worth it!)

If anything, try to *over* budget, rather than under budget. The last thing you want to do is get one month in, and realize that you're going to have to start eating nothing but microwave noodles because you didn't account for the higher food costs abroad. It will pay off to be a little more generous now, so you won't regret it when you return. Remember that being frugal and saving money now will only help you avoid stress later on.

How to stick with your budget

Sticking with your budget can be difficult for some students. This is mostly because there is a constant stream of unique activities, evenings out, and social engagements that you're going to want to participate in. Hopefully, you've *over* budgeted for your entertainment expenses, which will allow you to continually say "yes" when you're friends invite you to that Real Madrid game or the Italian Opera House.

The best way to stick to a budget is to create an effective, reasonable spending plan from the start. Knowing exactly how much money you have to spend (or cannot spend) each month will help you to mentally keep track of what you can and *really can't* do.

Here are a few extra money-saving ideas:

- Host parties or get-togethers at your house or dorm room, rather than going out. Ask each person you invite to contribute something to the snack bar or drinks cabinet.

- Get an International Student Identity Card, which will garner all sorts of discounts all over the place, from public transport tickets and museums to dining out at any local hotspot.
- When you travel, use budget options to get around and always ask about extra student discounts. (Just go to www.Ryanair.com or www.Easyjet.com to book your next trip for big money saving deals) Stay in hostels or dorm rooms rather than hotels.
- Cook! Along with the numerous benefits I mentioned in chapter 4 about cooking, doing this will also save you LOTS of money in the long run. Basically, if you're going to eat out, make it count.
- Go to all the events offered on campus. These functions often have complimentary appetizers and drinks for all attendees.
- Eat in the school Mensa or cafeterias. In many countries, university food and housing is heavily subsidized, meaning you can get a meal for practically nothing when you eat in the on-campus dining rooms.
- Be creative and find your own fun. Make a point of discovering the free things to do in

your area such as free museums, parks, walking tours, and beaches.

Scholarships & grants

There are literally thousands of scholarships and grants available to university students interested in studying abroad. All you have to do is find the right one for you. Your first point of contact for finding overseas scholarships should be your home university's international studies and financial aid offices. They will be able to point you toward any financial aid options from your local school.

The next stop should be websites such as www.StudyAbroadFunding.org and www.InternationalScholarships.com, which offer huge databases of scholarships available to study abroad students. You're going to need a head start on this process to ensure you get all that you need. It's advisable to start as early as a year in advance of your actual study abroad dates because some programs have early cut-off deadlines that must be met. Many of these scholarships are major or program-specific, and they often require you to fill out lengthy forms, write essays, and even do charity work during your time abroad. These can be worthwhile experiences by themselves if you have the right attitude going in. You'll receive the financial backing you're looking for while obtaining insightful knowledge about the group(s) you assist.

Working while you study abroad

Another option for sorting out money matters is taking on a job while you're abroad. This can be very beneficial, but sometimes difficult. First of all, if you're only studying abroad for one semester, finding a job in that short amount of time could be problematic. Secondly, some countries simply do not offer work permits to study abroad students.

To find out if you're eligible to work in your study abroad country, you'll need to consult a) the website of your destination country's embassy or b) the international office at your study abroad university-where professionals can advise you about the local laws and your rights as a student. Most often, international students are allowed to work part time (usually up to twenty hours a week) while studying abroad, but find out in advance so you don't break any laws. Remember that you are always expected to behave under the law of your study abroad country; know what you can and can't do in all situations.

Getting hired is the next challenge, and it's even trickier if there is a language barrier. However, working in your study abroad country is perhaps the single best way to improve your language skills in a short period of time. The top places to seek out a job as a study abroad student are in the service industry. Places such as cafes, bars, and restaurants provide the perfect platform for advancing your speaking ability. It is also possible to get hired by a local tour company as an English-speaking tour guide. This can be an incredibly fulfilling job to take on, but if you plan to pursue this type of work, you should make sure you are well read on the local history, sights, and customs.

Finally, be sure to consult Chapter eight of this book for advice on how to maximize your chances of getting hired by tailoring your resume to fit the local cultural expectations.

Financial Planning Notes

7. Health and Safety

Post-tourist bombings in Cairo, Egypt:

The week before departing to the third world
country of Egypt I found myself as apprehensive as
I've ever been in my twenty-one years of living, and
eye-opening in all ways possible. The startling news
of the previous weeks' Cairo bombings, past
kidnappings of Americans, and general barbaric

behavior that exists in this place caused a lot of commotion in the weeks leading up to our recession. In fact, of the forty or so of us that booked this trip, about twenty-five students canceled their excursions. I woke up early Thursday morning with the uneasy feelings that accompany those times in life where certainty is absent, and seemingly impossible to obtain again.

I took the liberty to find a hostel for us that had positive ratings, and a location that would cater to our extensive plans. Sean saw my list of things to do and commented on my obvious type-A habits. My overly analytic and careful tendencies were heightened this week. It was a gift and a curse I would say, but it certainly got the job done. Our entire group would be residing at the infamous Brothers Hostel, a place that had a flawless reputation in terms of preparing itineraries, drivers, and the best tour guides available. However I quickly discovered there were no spots left at Brother's, which seemed like a disaster at the time. Therefore, I decided to take a leap of faith and settle on a two-month old hostel: the City Plaza. I confirmed a driver for us once we arrived in Cairo, which chipped away at some of the anxiety I was feeling, printed my flight itinerary and said, "Here goes nothing!"

My first experience on an Arab flight was one of cognitive dissonance. After observing the Arab writings all over the pamphlets, signs, and food containers, I couldn't help but think of September 11th. It was a completely irrational thought... but it was still there.

Although despite some minor turbulence, and an airsick Egyptian man sitting next to me, the flight went by smoother than I expected. Especially considering there were many unusual procedures we were put through. Filling out several arrival cards so we could get our Egyptian visas and learning the currency conversion rates wasn't difficult to grasp, but it had to be learned quickly. This was because the locals were trying to sell me *toilet paper* the instant I got off the plane... just in case I needed to use the bathroom? That was something I was not expecting.

After going to the bathroom, you will notice there are no paper towels. Each morning, every bathroom in Egypt becomes a haven for savvy businessmen who see toilet paper as a valuable commodity. They guard the dispensers and treat their "jobs" as if they're selling their life's work. Of course, they're just waking up early to sell the toilet paper to people who really need it. Anything to make an *Egyptian pound* is fair game I guess.

We continued on and turned in all our assorted currency for Egyptian pounds, which was a very good exchange rate. As soon as we passed by the visa booths I saw a man with less than ten teeth holding a sign... *Connor LaVallie* it said. I hesitated briefly before shaking his hand as he shrieked... "Welcome to Egypt!"

The drivers in Egypt make the Roman drivers seem like sixteen-year-old kids trying to obtain their licenses on the day of their road tests. It was unreal... swerving, honking, and yelling has no limit in Cairo. Street signs for crossing are non-existent. I looked out and thought about what it would be like to attempt to cross the street. I decided it would feel like the arcade game, *Frogger...* only on these roads it would be *Frogger in hell.*

We arrived at our hostel and saw a little blinking sign that read "City Plaza Hotel." I'm sure the looks on our faces were priceless at this very moment because the first five floors looked like something out of a World War II movie scene. Additionally, there were infinite stray cats, dead bugs, rotten furniture, and an unpleasant odor I couldn't identify. Luckily for us, the sixth floor was the actual hostel area and it was immaculate. Just as we entered, a well-dressed man with big white teeth, a robustly gelled comb-over, and thick glasses greeted us with enthusiasm. He showed us to our sufficiently kept room and told us to come out and meet in the computer area when we got settled in.

This was where we met our man, Jamaica. He was a short, young, bald Egyptian guy who was there to discuss all we intended to see and experience while in the ancient city of Cairo. We booked our side-trips and felt content with everything we chose to accomplish. However our plans would not be final until we received the total cost and paid for it all. After about five minutes of bargaining, we accepted his price of 600 Egyptian pounds. This was a more than reasonable deal for a four-day trip all over Egypt.

Jamaica then gave us a solid recommendation. He described to us a local restaurant that we immediately sought out and found on the top floor of a shoe store. The incredibly conducive exchange rate allowed us to obtain just about anything we wanted in Egypt, and this was especially true when it came to the food. We proceeded to order courses of spiced salads, chicken shwarma, Egyptian pancakes (which tasked like funnel cakes), and olive leafs stuffed with meat and rice... all for about 3 USD per person. By end of the trip, we frequented this authentic restaurant about five different times while enjoying *real* Egyptian cuisine, becoming friends with the owner, and paying less than we would have at any fast food joint in the United States.

The next morning we had a driver take us to see the mysterious pyramids of Giza. We made our way through a narrow alley full of local people making ceramics, wandering stray animals, and the same unidentified odor of previous areas we visited. We came upon a little toothless Egyptian man as he greeted us kindly. He immediately asked us if we wanted camels or horses to take us to the pyramids. We unanimously chose to take camels, and then the bartering began. We worked this intense little guy for forty-five minutes taking his initial offer of 800 Egyptian pounds down to 200 pounds per person; we were getting the hang of this! We took dozens of pictures and enjoyed the slow, scenic ride to the pyramids. Through the bustling streets of beggars, merchants, tourists, and local school children... we finally reached our destination.

I had mixed feelings of both awe and disgust. The men trying to make a pound in any which way they can, constantly bugging you to buy this, do that, come ride my camel... I was surprised by the lack of dignity some people possess. However there are issues that run a lot deeper than most of us could fully comprehend in these places. The thieves, peasants, conmen, and policemen constantly hanging around the pyramids were pitiful. But seriously, who am I to judge?

In a place like this I couldn't help but think about my own life. All the things I have, the people around me, my family, and my home will never be taken for granted again. I felt this deep appreciation for the people in my life after witnessing how certain parts of the world live and operate. I think this is an important lesson for any westerner to learn after spending time in a developing region.

Our next stop was the train station. There was a remarkably old metro car that would take us eleven hours overnight to the holy city of Luxor. It was a one-room car with six ripped up chairs, two old white-haired Egyptian men, and two younger guys from Belgium. We passively competed for space and personal comfort on the long ride. The older guy next to me snored, which produced a noise that could have competed with the classic rock song playing on my iPod at full volume. However there was nothing that could distract my thoughts about the remarkable place we were headed.

The moment we arrived the next morning, our new tour guide greeted us. He explained that we were about to see all of what Luxor had to offer. *The Valley of the Kings* contained the tombs of Rameses IV, II, IX, Tutankhamen, and other ancient kings of Egypt. The tombs were truly awe-inspiring. The massive statues, extremely detailed hieroglyphic writing, and decorated corridors were beyond what I had imagined. The fact that this was all accomplished flawlessly before any of the modern technological advances we utilize today was astounding. This thought echoed through my head repeatedly on this journey through Luxor.

We saw many temples included Kataran; a place with pillars more massive than any two I've seen in Rome... combined. Our private tour guides really went out of their way to show us everything Egypt and Luxor had to offer. They couldn't have done better in terms of being on time, and keeping us informed about all that we saw. This made for an entertaining and educational experience that totally surpassed our expectations.

As night drew near, we were dropped off at a hotel with about four hours to spare before we would be picked up to go back to the train station. Compared to the Paris metro system, Egypt was a significant demotion in comfort. However we were enjoying the new perspective we gained on how people traveled in Egypt. The only concern was a lack of sleep the past few days. Therefore, our instincts told us to rent a room so we could potentially get a bit of shut-eye before the long night that awaited us ... but we decided to visit the Luxor museum instead. Aside from all the priceless exhibits and relics, the event that really stood out was when Sean asked a guard if we could take pictures of Rameses I mummy. There were "no picture taking" signs and guards all over, so asking for permission was the only way it was going to happen. The policeman agreed, but just before we left the display, the crooked guard leaned over and demanded a tip. We deleted our pictures after that. If you didn't *pay a toll,* you could be in serious trouble with the local law enforcement. This was something we decided to seriously avoid for obvious reasons.

On the train ride back we made friends with our South American car-mates and shared an Egyptian tea drink. One girl in our group had her backpack stolen right off her chest when she was sleeping on the way in to Luxor. We were told that this was a fairly routine occurrence on Egyptian train cars. It's best to sleep *on top* of your luggage she said. Just to be safe, that is what we did on the ride back to Cairo.

I was immediately put in charge of the group when the driver gave me the ticket for the six of us during the trek back. I was awakened several times during the night to show our ticket in order to prove we belonged on the train. One time I nearly dropped and flushed the ticket down the toilet. This would have resulted in the six of us getting kicked off in the desert, *somewhere* between Luxor and Cairo. However, we made it back safe, and only sixteen hours behind in sleep. But I can assure you it was all worth it.

The rest of the trip was much more revealing and educational as I developed more confidence in myself in terms of what I could endure and accomplish. We found ourselves in unknown areas around the city, far away from our hostel, while being scammed by a "school teacher" on our way to the Egyptian museum. He was actually working for a shop owner and tried to lure us into an unfamiliar building. However we continued to follow our instincts, which always proved to be the best course of action in Egypt.

Passing by the fake-shoe shops, doll stores, tourist traps, and everything in-between, sometimes left an uneasy feeling in me, and I found myself dreaming of Rome or Chicago. Even with these sporadic negative feelings, I felt immensely privileged for everything I witnessed and absorbed during those few days. At 5 o'clock in the morning everyday, the whole city prayed to Allah for the first of five times that day. It's moving to see how people so different from myself go about their lives. This was an important pillar of Islam, and they were proud to wake up by singing their prayers each and every morning under the rising Egyptian sun.

From the day I departed for Egypt, to the time we said goodbye to our hosts at the Plaza Hotel, I learned many incredible lessons. We remained safe throughout the trip and breezed through Luxor without a scratch. I learned that when it comes down to it, all of us are more similar than we believe initially. I really think every human being has the same needs; some people just go about fulfilling those needs differently based on their own unique background and perspective. When speaking of the Egyptians, I don't think we could be more different in that regard. The environment clearly shapes one's actions and beliefs, but at the core, we are very much the same. I'm glad I've found these answers here, of all places.

—————————

Staying Safe While You're Abroad

If your parents are like most; they're probably incredibly concerned about you staying safe while studying abroad. If you think you're invincible, you should check yourself and tread lightly. Safety is important to take seriously, but you definitely shouldn't obsess about it either. If you follow your instincts, use your head, and stay away from illegal and potentially dangerous activities... you're unlikely to run into any problems while you're overseas. However, there are a few things you must keep in mind *just to be safe.*

International Safety Issues

Being safe while you're abroad is a key concern for both you as a student and your family. In many cases you will find that most of the danger stories about going abroad are exaggerated, but crime can and does happen to students. Even though most students are checked for health risks before going abroad, medical issues can arise either through sickness or accidents. Thus, you should understand what you need to do, and where you need to go for help in case of an emergency:

- Leave valuables at home. There are some things that you really don't need while you are studying abroad. This includes expensive jewelry, fancy watches, and designer sunglasses. Also, any personal item that you would be heartbroken to lose should never leave home.

- Keep your belongings secure. There are multiple elements to this:
  - Keep cash, passports, cameras, and other valuables put away and out of sight in your room. Whether you are with a host family or are in a student-housing situation, reduce the temptation for cleaning staff, roommates, or extended family members to "clean up" on your behalf.
  - When you are out on trips, keep your belongings close. Keep backpacks zipped and don't let things hang out of your pockets.
- Be aware of your surroundings constantly. Keep track of where you are, even if you are having a night out on the town. Understand where bus lines or taxi connection points are in relation to you. If you're lost and you've had too much to drink, it's time to get back home. It just isn't worth the risk in unfamiliar territory.

- Travel in a group. In many cultures, traveling alone or going alone to clubs is not the norm for young people. Learn to travel with a companion for safety reasons, and to fit in. Even if this is counter to your naturally independent habits, you need to make this exception. This is especially important if you are a woman.
- Learn local medical symbols. Pharmacies are usually a first stop for minor health issues abroad. Knowing how to locate a pharmacy or identify local clinics can help you take care of your personal health for most problems.
- Know how to get an ambulance and locate the nearest local hospital. Thanks to online maps, you can pinpoint hospitals before you even arrive to any destination. Be the one in your group who has done the research, and knows where to go if something goes awry.
- Understand how to contact the local police. Look up the relevant numbers and have them handy.

You should know how to contact your home country's consulate. Your embassy can help you out of major emergencies, and also provide evacuation services during natural disasters. Many consulates ask you to register with the embassy when you arrive to ensure you are on their mailing list of residents to evacuate in the event of an emergency.

Consideration for Protecting your Safety

A great rule of thumb is to try and avoid making yourself look like a visitor. Certain activities are sure to paint a big red target on your back for criminals. These include:

- Pulling out wads of cash when paying for something
- Wearing expensive jewelry and accessories
- Checking your guidebook or map for a long period of time on the street
- Following strangers to an isolated location, for any reason
- Accepting a drink or other ingestible item from a stranger
- Leaving your drink or other ingestible item unattended at a bar or party
- Not knowing the laws of the country you're in

Let me give you one major piece of advice. Spend some time learning the local laws, for they could be very different from the laws back home. For instance, did you know that possession of marijuana could carry a death sentence in China? It is important to remember that you are susceptible to local laws, and if you break one, you could be in a lot of trouble. Sometimes we might think that just because we are foreigners, or students, we can plead ignorance and be let off easy. This will probably not be the case. Breaking a law ... no matter how trivial or antiquated it may seem to you, can be cause for severe punishment in that country. You could potentially get kicked out of your study abroad program, deported, or even imprisoned in worst-case scenarios. However all these things are easily avoidable, you just have to be careful and use your best judgment.

It's also important to remember that ideas about free speech and personal opinions are not necessarily the same all around the world. If you are open about criticisms of the government or the local culture, it could be very distasteful to your host family, local friends, or classmates. Sometimes, it will be necessary to keep your opinions to yourself. If necessary, write a journal outlining your thoughts, or get together with other like-minded students to discuss your feelings privately. Otherwise, be respectful of the way things are done in your study abroad country at all times.

How to avoid being….

...pick-pocketed

To avoid pickpocketing, always keep cash and valuables in your front pants pockets or in a hidden money pouch. *Always* keep an eye on your passport and never leave anything valuable in the external pockets of your purse or backpack. If you find yourself in a crowded area, check your pockets often and carry your backpack on the front of your body. Put your purse strap around the opposite shoulder to avoid having it snatched away. Be especially careful in train stations and Internet cafes, as these are particular havens of robbery. Don't ever leave your bags out of direct eyesight. Highly skilled thieves can take something right in front of your eyes without you even noticing.

At ATMs, always cover the keypad while entering in your PIN number and never allow someone to distract you while you are using the ATM. There have been incidents where one thief watched the PIN being entered from behind while another thief dropped a few notes of money on the ground. Thief 1 then told the ATM user that she dropped the money and when she bent down to pick it up; Thief 2 took her ATM card. Thus, the thieves had both the PIN and the ATM card and were not afraid to use it.

...scammed

Scammers can be pretty hard to spot if you are ill informed about their tendencies. They usually appear as fairly normal students, artists, or other friendly types of folks. They'll usually offer to show you around, or help you find and/or buy something. Scammers target people who look lost or don't seem to know what is going on. Their scams can take any form like trying to sell you some stolen art, or simply taking your wallet or purse. The general rule to remember is to be suspicious of most people on the street who offer you something, or seem friendly for no reason.

...taken for a "ride" in a taxi

The best way to avoid being scammed in a taxi is to have an idea of where you're going. I know, I know ... you probably *don't* know where you're going and that's *why* you got the taxi in the first place. However, the fact is: if you don't want to be taken advantage of, do not get into a taxi without knowing exactly where you're going and roughly how much the ride will cost. That means being able to confidently name the address, street, and neighborhood you're heading to, and having an outline in your head about how to get there.

In order to do this, you should study a map before getting in the taxi. Know the names of major streets that you should be passing, and the general direction you should be going. It's even better if you have an idea of some landmarks you might pass on the way as well. If you're worried, you should have the map open in the taxi to track your route. This will also let the driver know you're staying on top of things. If you suspect that a taxi driver doesn't know the way, or if they're improperly raising the tariff, don't be afraid to speak up and restate your directions/ concerns. Tell him which streets you would like him to take, or simply get out.

- Never agree to get into a taxi that doesn't use a meter unless you are extremely confident in your haggling skills and directions ~ OR if it's an emergency.
- Try to find out the telephone number of a local taxi reporting service (many cities have them) and call it if you feel in danger or if you feel like you're being taken for a ride.

...being a victim

If you follow the above advice, you're unlikely to become a victim. The idea is to learn to rely only on yourself for directions and information. Don't be too trusting of others no matter how friendly they might seem on the surface. Avoid walking around at night alone, or venturing into unfamiliar areas of a city before confirming whether they are safe. As a foreign student, you need to increase your awareness and learn to follow your instincts. No one can afford not to take this aspect of studying abroad seriously. However if you keep your eyes open and stay under the radar, you should have no problem with any of these issues.

Medical

Your study abroad program should give you some literature about what to do in case of a medical emergency. Since many countries run their health care systems differently, you should contact the international office at your study abroad university for the best way to get treatment. Most universities have an on-campus doctor's office or medical center that will treat students for cheap, or even for free. Obtaining the proper treatment you need should not be difficult. Therefore, even if you come down with something minor, consult a professional.

- Make sure you're covered with health insurance. Check with your provider to ensure that your coverage extends overseas, and if it doesn't, invest in a traveler's health insurance policy.

- Obtain copies of your medical records. If shots or records of immunizations are required for your destination, you will want to ensure that you have made the right appointments to have everything you need.
- Bring original copies of all of your prescription medications, as well as their original bottles in case you need to prove the prescription, or get it re-filled abroad.
- You should bring a first aid kit with some common medications. If you need to buy more abroad, it helps to know the generic names: Advil is *ibuprofen*, Bayer is *aspirin*, Pepto-Bismol is *bismuth subsalicylate*, Antacids are *calcium carbonate*, etc.
- Always know the name and phone number of a nearby hospital or emergency clinic in case you have a real problem.
- Put an "In Case of Emergency" contact into your cell phone, preceded by the letters "I.C.E." so that rescue/emergency workers know whom to contact on your behalf.
- My roommate was a member of a **medical assistance company.** This provided him with everything from access to vaccines and doctor referrals, to emergency evacuation services. Plans, packages, and options can vary, so be sure to check out http://

www.internationalsos.com/en/ and http://
www.travelassistance.com/ to find out more
about services and price options available.

Legal

This is worth repeating because it could make all the
difference in your experience if you make a mistake:
register yourself with your home country's Embassy in
whichever local country you're studying (you can do this
online) so if an emergency happens, they will already
have record of your presence in that country. If you
get into trouble, contact your Embassy for advice.
They will be able to provide information on how to
proceed in your situation. They will also arrange
legal help or representation if necessary.

Remember to make copies of important files just in
case you lose them. In the past, students were advised
to have physical paper copies of all their passports,
ids, visas, debit and credit cards for safety and
security reasons. Nowadays paper copies are still
acceptable, but you should also scan any important
documents like passports, credit cards, ID cards,
insurance cards, etc. and save those images in your
email account. They can be attached to draft emails
and sent for security, or you can have them saved as
Google documents to share with parents and friends
if needed.

Academic

For academic problems, your first point of contact should be your professors and advisors. They should be able to provide you with all the assistance and information you need about the courses you're taking, and any performance polices you should be aware of. If you're truly struggling, or have some kind of conflict with a professor, your best resource is the international office at your study abroad university.

Your program directors are used to dealing with students from all over the world, so chances are they will understand any of your concerns. Therefore, don't hesitate to go to them for advice about academic trouble. They can also work on your behalf if there is a cultural misunderstanding regarding academic work, or if you need more time to complete a project due to a cultural difference. The key to finding a solution is to be open about your problem, and communicate any difficulties you may experience with honesty and clarity.

Staying Healthy

Before you depart, you need to make sure of your own health considerations. Everyone's situation is different, but it's crucial to take the necessary steps to ensure you maintain a healthy mind and body while you're abroad. Disabilities and other health problems aren't necessarily a reason not to study abroad. However, having a pre-existing condition may require you to be more vigilant about your health while you're overseas. If you have a disability or health problem, consult with your university's study abroad office or a program advisor about your condition.

Your general health while studying abroad depends largely on your lifestyle and personal choices. In general, avoid activities that could jeopardize your health and vitality:

- Overeating
- Excessive partying
- Staying up when you're tired
- Binge drinking
- Taking any drugs you shouldn't be
- Eating only packaged, or fast food
- Sitting on your sofa *all day* watching soaps in a language you don't understand
- Not communicating your feelings to anyone (if you're homesick, burnt out, etc.)
- Eating or drinking things you're unfamiliar with, or allergic to (ask questions if you're unsure)

Getting Exercise

Many students are easily deterred by the fact that working out may be a lot harder to do while studying abroad. I decided to ask a well-respected athlete what his views are on the subject of studying abroad as an athlete and bodybuilder. Evan Centopani studied in Florence, Italy while in college and he disclosed some information that really made an impression on me:

"I went back and forth about whether or not to go to Italy and honestly, it is one of the best things I have ever done if not THE best. You will come back from it (if you ever come back) a better person having experienced another culture. Traveling in general is incredible. If you take one piece of advice from me, listen when I tell you to go. Bring as much money as you can and travel as much as humanly possible, it is worth every penny. It's one of the only things I would even consider being in debt for. The food is incredible all over Europe and the lifestyle is second to none, especially for an athlete.

I don't think I ever slept as much as I did in Italy or ate as well. Food and sleep, what more can you ask for? The ONE (and probably only) drawback is that finding a good gym over there will probably be next to impossible. You'll find one, but it won't be what you're used to at home. But I'm sure you'll be able to make do. Trust me, your sport isn't

going anywhere. Don't give it another thought. Go go go!
Just go."

Based on my experiences and the research I've done, I couldn't agree more with Evan. As athletes looking to make progress, or normal people just trying to maintain our waistlines... living abroad does pose a few problems. From the issues I discussed in previous chapters about finances, homesickness, and culture shock to the more distinct concerns such as the lack of a proper gym, solid nutrition, and lifestyle maintenance, just understand you *will* be able to cope with it all.

Finding a Place to Workout

Exercising while traveling isn't too tough. However I know there are many things you'd rather be out doing than running on a treadmill. But the fact remains, you cannot skip exercising altogether, or you're going to put on weight quickly from all that delicious foreign food you've been enjoying.

Depending on where you're staying, it can be a burden to find a well-equipped gym. The JFRC at Loyola had a fully equipped 24-hour fitness center, so I was lucky in that regard. The best thing you can do is search the area you'll be living in extensively before you leave. This way, you won't even have to think about it once you arrive. If you like to workout in gyms, you'll just have to face the fact that *most* of the world simply doesn't. You will not find the same cardio equipment, power racks, and barbells like you would in the United States. This can be hard to adjust to at first, but like Evan said, you will be able to find some type of standard place that has what you need.

Some universities may have a gym open to students for free, or a small fee. It might be worthwhile to invest in a membership and attend a couple days a week. If the weather is good in your country, make exercise into a sightseeing trip. Go for a weekend hike; take a run on a secluded beach, jog through a historic neighborhood, or cycle through the local farmland. Carry your camera on these journeys, and document what you see as you make it a true scenic adventure.

After you determine which form of exercise you'll participate in abroad, it would be wise to come up with a training strategy that will correspond to your travel arrangements and goals. It will be difficult to adhere to a comprehensive, high frequency fitness routine while studying abroad, so I recommend formatting your workouts a little differently to utilize your time most effectively.

- Decide how much time you and your travel partners can realistically devote to exercise during the week.
- Your schedule can vary substantially, so make sure to focus during the allotted time you have, and take complete advantage of your time in the gym.
- If you lift weights, keep your reps in the 6-10 range for most exercises to ensure you're going heavy enough to keep the muscle you have.
- Warm up! I can't emphasize this enough. There will probably be times when you've had a layoff and can't wait to get back in the gym... but don't rush it. Start out slow and always maintain correct form to avoid injuries. (Check out www.bodybuilding.com/exercises for tips on how to perform any exercise in the gym)

Even though you're studying abroad, and not *training abroad*, it would be foolish to recommend that you don't worry about working out. In fact, I think it should be one of the first things you research before arriving to your intended destination. Just don't let it control your decisions, or take priority over any other unique experience you come across. If you happen to miss a workout, that's definitely okay. Adjust your plan and keep moving forward.

Nutrition Advice for Athletes

As I discussed in Chapter 5, one of the best parts about living in another country is becoming acclimated to the local cuisine. However this can either make or break your fitness endeavors. Most countries' markets carry organic local produce, meats, dairy, and other specifics depending on your locale. This is fine when you're studying during the week, but what about venturing off to other lands? Here are a few ways I got around in the deserts, cathedrals, piazzas, museums, and away from the tenacious street vendors.

- o Invest in a protein supplement. Finding a decent dietary supplement shop is not for meek. The same can hold true for online orders as getting it through customs can be difficult. Instead, place an order of everything you need, and pack an extra suitcase before you leave home.
- o Carry some *instant oatmeal* and nuts. Any time you need to eat, mix up some oatmeal and throw some nuts

in with your protein powder. The instant oats float in the water and they're much easier to drink than the old fashioned kind. You can get oats or nuts almost anywhere for a balanced meal on the go.

o   Pack light when going on trips (for more on packing, refer to chapter 1). Wear your heavy clothes on the plane, and pack your food. You can always take off layers... you can't always get the food you need.

When you're traveling through unknown regions, having extra food with you is a great idea. You'll be glad you have the supplements when you're trekking through the streets of Rome or sleeping in the Sahara desert. Doing these little things will give you peace of mind, and make life easier when sitting down for a meal isn't possible. Once again though, in the grand scheme of things, you will not regret missing a meal or two. The people you'll meet, places you'll see, and events you experience will matter a lot more than getting a little out of shape. So don't stress.

Making the decision to study abroad as an athlete can be a very hard decision at first. Many athletes decide not to go at all because of many of the dilemmas I discussed above, which is a big mistake. In general, you might discover that your lifestyle abroad is actually healthier than at home. You'll probably walk and/or bicycle a lot more than normal, and the food you eat will likely be fresher and healthier than the typical western diet.

As an athlete, I was very apprehensive about going abroad, but it was one of the best things I could have ever done for myself. Part of the *Truth* is about sharing the same fears and uncommon adventures with people; it will bring you closer together. You will meet new life-long friends because of the times you've shared in these far away places. Your sport, hobbies, and talents aren't going anywhere, but the opportunity to maximize your college experience will be gone before you know it.

8. Making the Most of Your Experience

Close Calls of Tenacious Pursuit in Istanbul, Turkey:

As I sat there in my humble, half-dirty dorm room, surveying the four-month schedule before me, an overwhelming sense of urgency, relief, gratification, and skepticism was drowning me like a lonely, deserted camel... discovering quicksand.

Time management was of the essence in Rome. I was alone at Loyola University's John Felice Rome Center for the first time in over three months; it's been so long I forgot what quiet sounds like: I can tell you now, it felt liberating.

About a week earlier, I had returned from Turkey and I wanted to write a blog entry entitled, Planes, Trains, and Mopeds for our flight to *Istanbul,* train to *Florence,* and our second day-long scooter excursion through the *Eternal City.* However I never made the time, and the majority of my feelings, as well as topical memories had faded. Our unrivaled ability to get the most out of each minute on trips was achieved best in Florence as we "saw it all" in half a day. Florence was an absolutely stunning city with an authentic Italian feeling I haven't felt since going to Trento to stay with Sean's relatives.

Then, the following day I was still battling the "Roman plague" (which is basically just a sore throat and hyperglycemia from all the pasta) but I somehow found myself racing through *Via del Corso* on a moped in a place where death is fifty times more likely to occur on the road than Los Angeles or London... it was worth the risk.

Instead of sweeping through all the main tourist attractions, we sputtered off the beaten path to explore the villas and affluent neighborhoods set on a cliff... with a panoramic view of downtown Rome. After eight hours of weaving through traffic, simultaneously holding a map and taking pictures, we got back to the rental shop in Piazza Barberini with no less than a minute to spare before the owners closed down for the night. Close call, because if you're late you pay double the rental price! These "close-call" moments occurred so often that I could not help but think of divine intervention. This is because each time we've been in a situation like this; we were only one *decision* away from having an altogether different, or a much worse experience than we set out for. Our decisions shaped our adventures, and each time we could have just as easily been left in the dirt... literally. Yet, we always came out on top, relieved and gratified with our "luck". Okay, okay... let me give you a couple examples...

Istanbul

Arriving in another Muslim declared region had me anticipating I would be in the familiar perplexed state I had felt in Egypt and Tunisia, only ~ I felt the opposite in Istanbul. My personal space was still protected the second I got off the plane! No one was asking me for a tip after using a piece of toilet paper like they did in Egypt... And people had teeth. Well, a few at least.

The immaculate, modern airport was literally a breath of fresh air. I knew we would be in Istanbul for a relaxing weekend that would undoubtedly satisfy any need we had. Instead of the track-race, honking, dirt-filled, crapshoot highways of Cairo, the scene I viewed from the cab on our way to downtown Istanbul reminded me of something natural. There were long, unblemished concrete walkways along the freight-filled seas, flowers representing every color conceivable lined the roadways so perfectly, they almost seemed artificial. But this, reminded me of Chicago... I looked out as branches broke the sun into bright streaks of light on people as they jogged with their dogs, rode their bikes, and took naps under enormous green trees, it was Lake Shore Drive... *eerie* I thought.

Even when I say we have no plan for a particular trip before departing, there is always some central objective or goal to fulfill. From the beginning of our semester in Rome, Istanbul became synonymous with words like "amazing" or "unrivaled" followed by *Black Sea* and *Turkish* bath. So I made it a priority to leave some free time in our four-month schedule to

see the mysterious Black Sea, and the baths of
Turkey.

We finally arrived at our destination, but my first
impression of our little hostel owner man was not
very promising. From the first words out of his
mouth to the last... always came with a slur or
mumble about his hookah bar and pine nut tea he
wanted us to buy. He obviously was not too keen on
spending his time making sure we knew the right way
to the sea port, or what time anything we were
interested in seeing would close. This is very rare
because most hostels will do everything they possibly
can to accommodate you. We decided that this guy
just needed to be informed of our exact intentions,
this way there would be no reason our trip shouldn't
work out perfectly.

Through his frequent murmuring, I gathered enough
information that would hopefully get us to our place
of interest: Asia, and the Black Sea. We traversed
around the closed-in streets, over the tram-tracked
road, through the stunning Blue Mosque (also
known as the Vatican of the Muslim world) across
carpet weaving stalls, in between kabob venders,
until we saw our destination: a string of grayish, rusty
ticket houses hungry for vanity-driven' tourists to

fork over their Lire for a chance to see Asia (or just to say they've been to Asia).

We anxiously approached the ticket booth with the optimism that comes with months of "good luck." I bellied up to the bench and confidently asked the dark-skinned, black bearded guard:

"One student- ticket to Black Sea?"

The look of puzzlement on the guards face immediately filled me with uncertainty, as his reply would confirm...

"Sorry, no English, next station... BYE" and that was it... no further information, or clarification on anything.

That should be simple enough I thought, the second station would have tickets. But just as I turned to leave... a short, unshaven, fat Turkish man with a notepad in his hand clutched my shoulder and asked...

"Black Sea?! Sorry, but boat don't run today, only tomorrow" my attention was suddenly diverted toward this strange fellow.

He immediately began his sales pitch, "I have boat, it is small... only fit ten people, four hour trip... and for you, good price, you have nice face."

Although he was creepy, he still had our attention. He proceeded to pull out a weathered travel map of the region with pen markings outlining his intended route for us.

"You see... we go to bridge, we stop for picture and you take tour of city... we stay for one hour half, and we come back here, no charge for cab, my son take you to boat... NOW, we leave two minute."

At this point, his proposal actually sounded reasonable, after all there was no possible way we could go to the Black Sea, this guy told us it was only running tomorrow!

"How much?" I asked...

"For you... seventy Lire, original price, one hundred twenty Lire, but we must go NOW!"

One thing I've learned in places like these, or anywhere else for that matter, is that anytime someone is hurrying you to pay money, or make a commitment that requires conscious reasoning, it is better to walk the hell away. So that's what we did. But the man scurried after us...

"Okay, okay... 50 Lire a piece", we keep walking... "Okay... 40 Lire for one!" He exclaimed

We stopped and thought about it. That's about 30 USD, a very reasonable price for a day trip around the coast of Turkey, on a private boat no less. But something was off, and we knew it. So we stuck to our gut, and told him "Le Shokran" (Arabic for no thank you) and we proceeded on toward the next station while simultaneously fighting off the desperate salesman.

The second grayish rust-crusted ticket house was like déjà vu, as the man behind the mirror had not a clue what we were talking about. He ordered us to leave the booth as our hopes of making it to the Black Sea left us as well.

We frantically began to search out someone, anyone who may be able to understand us, and give a little direction in the absence of our awesome hostel owner man. Through a sea of Turkish folk, we heard someone ask,

"Black Sea?"

This was our final burst of hope, and it came in the form of two grungy looking British guys. One was wearing white sunglasses and the other with a beard and clothing that allowed him to fit in with the locals.

They were directed to the third station, about eighty yards away…

"Leaves in one minute!" the British man yelled to us

We darted out, said a quick "thank you", and made it to the ticket stall and retrieved our prize… a six hour trip all over the Turkish coast, through the famous bridge that crossed into Asia, a pass through various fishing villages, and a three hour stop at the famous Castle city where we would use every minute to the fullest. We immediately bought twenty-ounce grilled fish sandwiches for 4 Lire as I witnessed a grey-haired jolly fat man filet, pick the bones, and wrap them up for us right on the water front. The rest of the time was spent atop the mountain-village next to an ancient castle. After taking several pictures, I found a patch of grass overlooking the Black Sea. I had to just stop, sit down, and think about everything and how lucky we'd been.

We made it back just in time to catch the boat back to Istanbul. On this night, we had only one goal... get a *Turkish bath*. This time, though, we wanted to make sure we knew exactly where we were going. We sought the help of our sharp-as-a-tack hostel guide, Mohammad, and asked him where we can get the best bath in Istanbul. He told us of one Hamam not too far away, and it would be open till Midnight. This was great we thought. On our last night we could relax, get some Turkish omelets, and not have to get there until around 10 PM... plenty of time.

Our plan was perfect; we had made it out of the Black Sea trip relieved and content once more in a close-call morning that couldn't have been spent in a more preferable manner. However, we decided to depart from *Backpackers* Hostel just a little early since we had everything done for the day. We made our way out with impeccable directions and the tensions built up after a long day... ready to be softened by a relaxing, authentic spa experience.

We stumbled upon a sign that read, "Cagaloglu Hamam...300 year old Turkish bath, as seen in the New York Times best seller: 1,000 PLACES TO SEE BEFORE YOU DIE" wow, we thought... just what we needed.

We eagerly stepped through an entryway that was enshrined with the acclaim of 300 years past. We were greeted at the door by two old men wearing white robes and expressions of confusion written all over their faces.

"Hello, what do you need?" the old man asked

I once again, confidently replied "We are here for a bath... how much" I asked

He laughed and said... "It is 9:15, we close at 10PM!"

My heart sank, I felt sick and thought my Turkish omelet was about to return. That was until he said:

"Usually 45 minutes is all you need, but you must hurry, come on!" The old man instantly turned into the Tasmanian devil as he prepared our robes, and centuries old wooden changing rooms. He handed me a three-pound key and brought me a beer, "The best in Turkey!" he told me.

I put on my crimson Turkish bath-towel, my two sizes too small wooden slippers, tucked my *dead skin exfoliater* into my pocket... and headed out to a bath where Constantinopolitan kings unwound after a strenuous day of ordering death and destruction in other lands.

Upon entering the Hamam, I was taken aback by the shining white marble that covered every inch of the ancient room; there was one enormous marble island in the center of the area, surrounded by little forever-running fountains. There were three men finishing up their services, so I followed the old man's orders and took my beer into the steam room (only in Turkey, I thought) I overlooked the festivities below to try and see what this would be like. Before I could close my eyes to relax, a thirty something year old Turkish man with a gold chain, and belly the size of beach ball entered. He started sputtering broken English all over the place. Among other things, he said he comes to this Hamam every week and always finds "*Rambo Americans*" (whatever that means) on the weekends trying to get a taste of the "good life". I thought to myself, 1) Mind your business, and 2) Good life? This is great, but man... if you only knew.

My turn was next. I stepped up on the marble island and got beat up for a solid thirty minutes straight. Elbows, forearms, and knees all are fair game as the *bath guys* use whatever they need to give a sufficient beating. The rest was scrubbing away on the skin with soap and hot water along with various back and neck cracks, most of which were done so quickly I couldn't think about the possibility he might make a mistake.

It all went by in a flash, but I had that satisfying jelly-like feeling your body gets after a massage. Those times when you're ready to collapse, when you're in a state of complete restfulness... that's how Turkish baths make you feel. I got washed up; tossed the other half of my beer down the drain, and found a goody bag in my changing room with boxer shorts, newspaper articles about the famous bath, wash cloths, and various Turkish mints and sweets. I thanked our gracious hosts, and noticed the clock read 10:30. They stayed open a half hour past closing time for us, so I tipped him and left with another "close-call" moment turned heavenly ... to tuck away and appreciate forever.

——————————

This trip became the culmination of many lessons Sean and I learned in the previous months. Before departure, we came up with a plan and a list of goals to accomplish in Istanbul. This really fueled our desire to make the most of our experience because the list was always there to remind us of our objectives. We made the weekend count, and finally made it back to Rome with another very successful journey behind us.

Make The Experience Count

So, you're all set to go. Keep yourself safe, eat new things, and take control of your life while studying abroad. But what is the point of it all? Undoubtedly, the idea is to have an amazing, unique, and life changing experience. What I'm saying is that you don't just want to just *handle* your life abroad; you want to *thrive* in it. Make the very most of it. Extract every lesson and life-changing moment you can from it as you go.

Another part of the *Truth* is that a study abroad experience will be the trip of a lifetime if you stay strong, smart, adventurous, and practice the suggestions in this book. Be sure to prepare the right materials before you go in order to avoid stress, and live each moment to the fullest. You'll want to take notes about your experiences in a journal so you will be able to remember every little detail when you get home.

Here is the secret:

Be in the moment

Look around you. Take closer notice of everything. Smile. Laugh. Cry. Shout. Feel intensely and express yourself. Talk to people, both the ones you like, and the ones you don't like as much. Taste *everything* (same rules from above apply) Learn to speak another language, and **step outside your comfort zone.** Feel the sun on your face and the rain on your skin. Take many photos. Write. Realize you may "know less," but appreciate more than ever. Watch as your opinions evolve, and your personality molds into something better. This, my friends, is what traveling is all about. And you're going to have a front row ticket... and back stage access to all of it when you study abroad.

Engaging people to help you

There are a *lot* of people available to you. We've talked about them in previous chapters. Professors, international office advisors, program managers, classmates, roommates, and friends can all provide a helping hand. *Use* them and let them use you. Learn to ask more questions, and make fewer assumptions about everything. Make suggestions and find out more about whatever intrigues you. When in doubt, always, *always* contact someone to help you out. Set up a language exchange to enhance your skills. Offer to volunteer for a day of charity work to see if you like it. Sit on a student committee. Vote in local elections if you can. Go to every university and class-sponsored outing that you're invited to, and talk to as many people as possible. If you get a weak answer, try somewhere else. And keep trying until you figure it out — whatever *it* may be.

Taking risks

Part of the process of becoming a better person is reaching out and stretching yourself to do things that aren't always within your normal routine. Now, I'm not saying that you should immediately go sign up for the first base jumping class available, but I am. What I mean is, you should take it slow at first and feel your way around your brand new environment with a few "comfortable risks."

Comfortable risks are things that might not be among your normal activities, but they don't scare the hell out of you either. Leaving to go study abroad is a comfortable risk, so congratulations, you're a big step ahead of your homebound classmates. But now that you're out there, you can't just sit back with the same type of routine and people you already know. You have to try out some new ventures. For many students this might be sampling a new type of food, or learning a new cultural hobby. For others, it might be stepping out into the vast unknown to work in a foreign restaurant, or heading to Switzerland to go skydiving above the Alps. For others, comfortable risks could simply mean talking to new people.

To be quite honest, it doesn't matter *what* comfortable risks you take, it just matters that you take them. I promise you'll get a thirst for the adventure once you experience the things that stretch you. Quit falling back on what's comfortable when you feel out of your element, and try something ~ anything ~ new. Once you develop a desire for these mini-risks, you'll become more and more open to bigger risks and challenges- even life changing ones. I'm not saying you'll necessarily turn into a skydiver, or want to swim with sharks, but you will be capable of taking in new information and handling whatever comes your way. In the end, that is what studying abroad is all about.

Getting an adventure partner

One way to make comfortable risks seem more possible is to hook up with a partner. No, not to have a one-night stand ~ but to find a friend that you can count on to do these new tasks with you. Ideally, this should be someone that you get along really well with, and hopefully they'll truly understand what you're going through as a foreign student in _____ (fill in the blank). The best place to find a proper friend is probably in one of your current classes, and it may require some work. You can't just show up and hope that someone approaches you — you've got to be proactive and take the initiative to find someone compatible with you. I realize, for some, this act in itself might represent a huge risk. However the rewards will be enormous, so have some faith and give it a shot!

Journaling & Blogging

Keeping a journal or a blog is an ideal way to document your travels and experiences; both for you and for your loved ones back home. It's best to keep your journal as up-to-date as possible lest you forget the feelings, sights, and smells of a particular day's events. I've found that journaling or blogging at night is usually the best time for remembering all of that day's encounters.

Why keep a diligent record of all these details as soon as possible? You're going to forget them, and you will appreciate putting in the work after you're home for a couple months. You will be able to look back and re-create the exact moments you had studying abroad. I know it may seem as though you'll never forget them. But believe me, even the intense memories will eventually fade. So take the time, and record your thoughts, reactions, reflections, and emotions in all situations. It will be a lot of fun to look back on those moments ten years from now and be able to remember everything.

Blogging and writing can also be a solid addition to your resume, and a way to break into a travel writing or journalism career if that is appealing to you. Look for local backpacker magazines, or certain language publications that might be interested in your stories. Even if they aren't openly hiring writers, it never hurts to approach a publication or website with your resume and a writing sample. Sometimes the best positions aren't even advertised. If you are willing to contribute a few interesting stories or blogs for free, you could potentially garner a few paid writing gigs. This may end up being a gateway to a later career, or just an extra stream of income while you're still earning your degree.

Show appreciation

Perhaps the most crucial thing you can do is to show appreciation to those around you for all the help, time, and friendship they've provided along the way. Go back to Chapter three and remind yourself of the cultural guidelines you've learned about. How do people show appreciation and say thanks? You want to show your gratitude in a way that's culturally appropriate. That way you won't embarrass, or unintentionally hurt the people that have showed you so much kindness. Gifts, tokens of appreciation, compliments, and quality time can be great gestures depending on the cultural context.

If you're invited to parties or dinners at others' homes, *do not* arrive empty handed. Small gifts brought by visitors are appreciated in almost every country around the world, so think of something small and appropriate ~ perhaps a dish you've cooked, a photo, or a memorable object that will make your host understand how much they mean to you.

Spend some time with the people that went out of their way for you, or put up with some of your idiosyncrasies. You'll know who these people are when the time comes to give back. Cultural lines around friendship can be very different, or even complicated. But if you work to understand where your local friends and acquaintances are coming from, you'll be able to make a great impression when all is said and done.

Now, put down the book, get outside, and make the most of your travels! Time is ticking and before you know it, you'll be back at home longing for the exotic streets, sights, smells, and tastes of your study abroad country.

It will easily become a time you'll always treasure. My roommate and I traveled to Egypt, Istanbul, Paris, Madrid, Greece, Switzerland, Tunisia, Sicily, and all over Italy. We both gave a speech at the end of the semester banquet based on Loyola's motto "Preparing people to lead extraordinary lives" which was like a dream when I think about it now. You will probably return home with a new appreciation for the world and the diverse cultures that exist in it. I certainly hope I never forget the lessons I learned and times I had in these places.

After returning home, my roommate contacted me about continuing what we started while studying abroad. He informed me about a China summer program and I instantly starting researching it. I was so excited I couldn't go to sleep that night. I began reading anything I could get my hands on about China and the culture. I knew that going to China was only possible because I made the most of my time studying abroad. I was interested in going further, and capitalizing on what I learned as a student overseas in Europe.

9. Capitalizing on Your Study Abroad Experience

Learning where we stand in Xi'an, China:

"Traveling through China with nothing more than a study visa and a few changes of clothes is freaking insane" I was told...

"You'll need a little of that Irish luck of yours to get through this one" another friend said. Even though I'm not sure either of these crass individuals had ever been outside the United States, their words proved to carry some value in the end.

A wise man once said to me "Luck is for the ill-prepared." When I think about that statement, I have to project myself exactly back to when Sean and I prepared to leave the disheveled region of Xi'an by railway.

As a Marketing and Finance major, Sean made a quick correlation to our transportation schedule...

"This is completely an *entrepreneurial* endeavor, there is a lot of risk in booking our trains, flights, tours, and every other event ahead of time like this... if one thing goes wrong, all those tickets are worthless and we lose an entire visit. However this seems like the perfect set-up if it all works out" I knew he was right, but being a self-proclaimed adventurer, I thought it would all work out or we'd just somehow find a way.

We never thought luck would be needed as long as things were planned, options were discussed, and sensible action was consistently taken. Upon waiting to depart from our hostel in Xi'an, we didn't have any resources to help predict our outcome however. The Internet was down, everyone around us spoke only Mandarin, and our maps were scattered with symbols completely foreign to us.

I gazed out the window... thunder started to rumble. I looked at my watch- ninety minutes before the train leaves... I looked at my half-packed luggage- where was my hand sanitizer? It only takes ten minutes to get to the station; we're all good I thought.

"We should get out of here, let's go catch a cab before this storm comes" Sean suggested.

"Good idea, let's get to Shanghai!" I replied.

We hoisted our two month's worth of baggage and proceeded to the massive double metal doors leading out to the street. We thanked our hosts and waved goodbye, fully expecting never to return... even though I knew we weren't fully prepared to leave. We stumbled outside, and turned the corner. Then to my horror, we witnessed the once desolate streets as they instantly filled with buses, scooters, occupied taxis, construction equipment, and every other motor vehicle known to man. It must be rush hour I thought.

All I know is there cannot be any other place on Earth where this title *rush hour* carries more accuracy. A deep, thick brown cloud of fumes filled the night air, and quickly engulfed my senses as we scurried to the nearest corner where taxis could see us. The ever-expanding population was in full display on the roads, and I was instantly reminded that pedestrians never have the right of way in China. I dodged a mafia-owned black Audi a5, almost losing my bag... and leg at the same time.

After almost witnessing death, Sean calmly stated "its okay, it only takes a few minutes to get to the station"... my type-A anxious tendencies must have been showing by now I thought.

"You're right; I'm just surprised none of these empty cabs are stopping." I said

Just then, a 5-foot nothing, nicely-dressed man holding a large umbrella came over and said to us in broken English:

"Taxi no stop here... go wight down this road... where you from?"

We told him thank you while dodging his subsequent questions, and continued through the frantic maze until we found another place to stop. Nothing was there. Maybe this corner?! Nada. I glanced at my watch: twenty-five minutes before departure. Soaked from the unrelenting rain, and thinking about our etched- in-stone schedule, I started to worry.

That was until our savior appeared. A taxi was empty and had actually stopped for us! He pulled up right beside me. I leisurely walked to the passenger window and asked him to pop the trunk. He glanced at our heavy cargo, then up at our matted wet clothes, and immediate sped off. He left us in the middle of the road in one of the most impoverished and densely populated cities in China during a rush hour storm. All this with only twenty minutes before our train to freedom would leave.

My pace quickened, Sean remained unusually calm considering the circumstances.

"Let's go back to the hostel and call a cab ... there's obviously some underlying agenda being carried out, or rule we're not aware of" I suggested.

Sean reluctantly agreed. We had already been running through the heavy rains since leaving our hostel some seventy minutes ago... but now I was sprinting. Sean yelled out that we were going the wrong way. I knew that he had a keen sense of direction, but I had to disagree this time. In the state I was in, all senses were heightened... including the one that brings the right answer in times of desperation and uncertainty. He caught up, but before we had a chance to discuss our next move, we saw it: A lone taxi had just pulled up about thirty meters ahead with no visible customer seeking a lift. Without hesitation... the race to get a ride began. We dug deep and burst toward the little green vehicle. We were finally going to have a chance to make it out of here!

Just then, a woman appeared about ten meters ahead of us, heading toward the same taxi. Stepping out in front of us was a twenty-something Chinese woman with long black hair, a designer umbrella, and high heels. She inched her way toward the driver side window in the nick of time to get her ride. Although neither of us said it at the time, I'm sure we were both thinking the same thing "Better her than us..." Oh well, this was it, game over.

But then, in utter disbelief, I watched her turn around and walk back toward the bus stop. We took one look at each other and *sprinted* back. The taxi driver motioned toward the meter... it was broken. This was a cab for hire now. He was looking to bargain and that was good I thought because I'm looking to spend!

To put it very lightly, the thought of spending another night in Xi'an was not only undesirable, but it would essentially ruin our entire schedule. I eagerly held up one hundred Yuan (about 12 USD) and showed him the map written in Chinese with our intended destination. For one hundred Yuan, this guy would be willing to take us to Russia if we wanted, but all we needed was a supposed ten minute ride to the train station. And we made this *very clear*. But we only had six minutes. He smiled greedily as we got in the taxi. He took off weaving through traffic as if his life depended on it. Ignoring the little men playing cards in straw hats, women carrying "fresh" water from the rain, and children dancing in the puddles on the streets... my heart pounded. We were traveling through the back roads, a part of Xi'an neither of us had seen before.

"Well if we don't make it... at least we got the scenic route" I offered.

Neither of us were in the mood for jokes, but we had to laugh anyway knowing how extreme the last hour and a half had been. Walls of people parted for the tenacious taxi driver. Through tiny streets barely large enough to accommodate the three-seated dune buggy of a car, we caught some air over a speed bump. Then, just over a few muddy hills, we saw it. Our final destination was now within reach. Our *go-cart* came to a screeching halt just before knocking a group of passengers over like they were human bowling pins.

I thanked our gracious/insane/greedy taxi driver and threw the one hundred Yuan at him as if it were just a few dirty pieces of paper. We jolted out the back seat and dodged through hoards of travelers until we found ourselves staring at the middle of the security line. The line wrapped all the way around the outside of the station, with no end in sight. There were 2 minutes left before our train would leave.

190

Just before all hope was lost... a thin, unshaven man wearing a conductor's hat motioned for our attention. We sauntered over, expecting the standard protocol... customs check, visa verification, etc. Then out of nowhere, he smiled up at us... and asked us:

"English?"

"Um, yes." we replied...

"Where you from?" he asked

"The United States." we answered

He suddenly smiled revealing his gold teeth and unexpected intentions for us. He began escorting us through the rain, past the *last minute* noodle vendors, in between patient locals, and finally to the front of the security line. Stunned, we presented our passports and had them stamped "Xi'an customs." We didn't ask any questions.

"Sank you!" he exclaimed.

With less than a minute left, we boarded our train en route to Shanghai. I collapsed on the seat feeling a little drained, somewhat guilty, and very content as I thought about our ill-prepared plan that somehow turned out perfect... and one of the luckiest days of my life.

_____

As I mentioned before, it isn't mandatory to have the perfect roommate or travel partner, but it definitely helps. Sean and I decided to take this post-undergraduate journey through China since we meshed so well while living in Rome. We talked extensively about the risks and potential rewards of experiencing the Far East. In the end, it became a quest for personal growth and unique knowledge to apply to our future careers in the "real world" back home.

Turn your new knowledge into reward

I can't stress enough how important it is to keep a record of your experiences. Creating a memory book will help you reflect back on your time abroad, and it will help you when you go to interview for jobs. Many people never have the chance to study abroad, so if you're able to talk about your experience effectively, it will make a strong impression with employers.

Having study abroad experience on your resume can create some unique opportunities for you. International experience, knowledge of one or more foreign languages, the ability to adapt, and understanding a foreign education system are all attractive qualities that will impress potential employers. However, you must know how to present them on your resume.

If you plan to work while you are abroad, or if you want to land a job after you finish your studies, there are a few things you should be aware of. First of all, in many foreign countries ~ especially other English-speaking countries, a resume is often referred to as a "curriculum vitae", or CV for short.

There are also many cultural considerations that go into creating a solid resume or CV, as every culture expects to see different information on one. For instance, in China, it is commonplace to put your parents' occupations and your age at the top of your resume. However, in the U.K. and Ireland, CVs tend to feature longer paragraphs describing your work history. Furthermore, American style resumes are usually filled with bullet points instead of long descriptions. The best way to make your resume look culture-specific is to ask a friend, classmate, professor, or advisor for advice on the type of formatting you'll need.

Spicing up your resume

When thinking about how to present your study abroad experience on your resume, you will want to consider how it relates to your chosen career path or intended job. For example, are you interested in business? Then you should *highlight* how your foreign language skills could benefit you in international business, or with foreign clients. This knowledge can apply to almost any career path, but it is up to you to decide how your study abroad experience can enhance your specific skills in the job market.

You will want to feature your study abroad experience under the "Education" section of your resume, first and foremost. Be sure to highlight any unique classes you took, any awards you might've received, and your relative grade point average. Of course, many foreign universities do not use the GPA system, but most of them will offer study abroad students an equivalency sheet for transferring the grades they received overseas.

Did you work while you were studying abroad? If so, you will want to include that experience under the "Employment History" section of your resume, *in addition* to the "Education" listing. Even if you simply waited tables at a café, or tended a bar, this will still set you apart from most applicants. Highlight any managerial duties you might have had, and relate how your foreign language skills played into your job. Additionally, think of creative and/or extra tasks you were assigned to because of your exclusive position as a foreigner.

In general, the best way to create a resume is to be empathic. Think about how you would view your resume if you were in charge of hiring someone for the same job you're applying for. You should also study the specific job listing in depth. Make sure to take notes on the specific requirements and qualities they are hoping for in a candidate. Which of your experiences fit into those categories, and why are they so unique? Why should you be given the job over someone else with similar experiences? Thinking about these critical questions will really help to maximize your chances of securing your desired position.

What types of jobs can I get?

Another part of the *Truth* is, a study abroad experience really is incredibly useful in almost any job market. Not only will it give you an edge, but it will also supply you with the necessary tools you need to excel in your career. However the *types* of jobs you'll be eligible for depend more on your chosen path of study at your home university. Therefore, you're study abroad experience will be more of an enhancement to your resume, rather than the sole selling point.

With that said, if you are majoring in foreign language, international business, intercultural studies, communication, or education, your study abroad experience will play a larger role in helping you secure a job. Studying overseas will be viewed as having an advantage in one of these fields, and it will impress employers if you can talk passionately about the ways it's helped shape your character. A genuine expression of your true passion will go a long way.

The types of jobs you can get with study abroad experience range from import/export management, being a manager in a multi-national corporation, to teaching English as a foreign language. How do you think your study abroad experience applies to your career goals? The way you answer this question will help you discover the path that's right for you. In fact, the world is in your hands... all you have to do is make a *decision* about what you want, and pursue your goals with hard work, consistency, and passion.

Using international experience to get hired

When going in for an interview, hiring managers may not express as much enthusiasm as you hope. Just because your study abroad experience is listed on your resume, doesn't mean you're guaranteed anything. However this does not mean they're not impressed. You will have to learn how to sell yourself. Just like a college degree doesn't guarantee you riches, an international study experience won't ensure employment. However, your chances for succeeding increase dramatically when you master both of these endeavors.

Before an interview, study the company's mission statement. Think about what each criteria means and how you and your experiences can fulfill it. Sometimes it might seem like a stretch, but there were experiences you've gone through while studying abroad that you probably don't even realize are useful and salient. Tasks like handling your student visa, sitting on an international student committee, seemingly unrelated hobbies, extra travel, and anything else you did in addition to studying will all be very important.

The question simply remains: *how you will convey this to your evaluators, and how will you convince him or her that these experiences are going to benefit you as a future employee?* The good news is that this is all up to you. I say *good news* you will have a whole new set of untapped tools and confidence you've obtained while living overseas. Knowing that you thrived in a challenging environment will bring out the enthusiasm your employers are looking for in an applicant. You will make a much larger impact on employers than the applicant who only has stellar grades and played flag football. Employers know what type of student takes on the challenge of studying abroad. It is a process that requires a lot of thought, self-discovery, time, and commitment to a goal. This is exciting, and anyone you talk to will begin to notice this.

It's simply outstanding to know that *you* have become a self-reliant adult with the capability to take whichever path you choose in life. Make the jump, take the risk, delve into the unknown, and prepare yourself to *lead an extraordinary life* after your study abroad journey. You may even discover yourself, and a whole new vision for your life while you're abroad.

Take what you've learned home with you, and don't stop until you've reached your dreams... then keep going.

10. Never Settle for Mediocrity

The Hunt for the Quanjude Roast Duck in Beijing, China:

1000 Places to See Before You Die. Check.

Fodor's See It China. Check.

The English-to-Chinese translation gadget. Check.

Two guys without a clue of where they were going, each equipped with a travel backpack and intent to live, breathe, understand, and experience *Planet China*. Check.

Connor and I were prepared for the unknown in an impromptu foreign expedition at its finest. We were confident in facing any challenge that arose even though we had *only* mastered two Chinese words, "Xièxiè" (Thank you) and "Ni hao" (Hello)... But were we really?

While browsing the book *1000 Places to See Before You Die*, Connor and I instantly spotted the Quanjude Peking Roast Duck. We admittedly both had an untamed curiosity and appreciation for exotic foods. Located on Qianmen West Street, the Quanjude restaurant was acclaimed as Beijing's largest roast duck restaurant, specializing in the ancient art form of cooking roast duck, dating back to the Yuan dynasty (1206-1368). Only the fruit of wood trees, such as date, peach, and pear, are used in the roasting process to give the meat a unique flavor, and the skin of the duck is made soft and crisp to melt in your mouth. Being the protein-enthusiasts we are, our jaws dropped at the proposition to kick off our Chinese adventure with such a feast. And our culinary expectations were sky-high. A hearty authentic Chinese meal sounded like the perfect way to relax after the arrival flight from the United States!

Ecstatic to begin the China adventure, and famished from the 13-hour flight from Chicago to Beijing, we discussed the first plan of action while at the Capital International Airport. We equally shared a sense of excitement to get into Beijing in spite of weariness from travel. We agreed to first take care of our hostel reservations, get settled in, and then head over to the Quanjude restaurant. Connor quickly made his way to the taxi stand while I went to the ATM to have my first encounter with the Chinese Yuan. I would have preferred to receive currency through my traveler's checks but the banks were closed (I secured quite a few traveler's checks from AAA a month before to avoid an international withdrawal fee from the ATM). But I soon realized that the local banks and money exchange bureaus charged a transaction fee for using the traveler checks – and that was just as high as the international withdrawal fee! Contrasting the easy accessibility of ATM machines with the difficulty of locating Chinese banks made it clear that ATM machines were the way to go.

By the time Connor arrived at the taxi stand, he had already flagged down a cab. We threw our luggage in the trunk, jumped into the back seat, and were oddly stared up and down by the driver (it must have been because we are both 6'3" and 220 pounds; much larger than the average local). That stare was a look that we became quite accustomed to...

Connor directed, "Leo Courtyard Hostel" in a clear voice that was slow enough for a Beijing-native to understand.

The cab driver sounded confused as he muttered, " Ni hao. Eh?" Connor and I looked at each other, dumbfounded that taxi drivers couldn't speak a shred of English.

Stage one of cultural shock hit us, confirming what an exhilarating challenge this trip was going to be. Luckily, the English-to-Chinese gadget came to the rescue by generating distinct, curvy characters in translation of Leo Courtyard Hostel. After twenty minutes of uncertainty, and a helpful call by the cab driver to the hostel, we finally began moving forward.

As the cab ventured closer and closer to the heart of Beijing, it became more apparent why author Maarten Troost coined the country *Planet China*... It was literally a different planet. The highway transformed into narrow stone roads that turned into twisting pathways entering the *Hutongs* (residential alleyways that are most common in Beijing). As the cab squeezed through the street corners, the *Hutongs* unfolded into street shops, barefoot children playing, small shacks, and men with rolled up shirts that exposed their protruding stomachs. What truly struck me was the acceptable cultural practice for the children to relieve themselves in the streets. This invariably contributed to an overwhelming smell in the air. At that moment, we both knew that any thought of luxury was out the window. The cab finally stopped after thirty minutes at the curtained entranceway of the Leo Courtyard Hostel.

As we walked into the musty little lobby, we were welcomed by two hostel employees. Barely able to see over the counter, Connor and I decided they couldn't have been more than sixteen years old. With smiles that lit up the dark and dreary halls, they walked us up to our room. Inside were two floor mats, two pairs of sandals for the bathroom (the bathroom floor wasn't completely clean), and, surprisingly, two beers to cool us from the heat.

Famished, we decided to head out to our Beijing destination, the Quanjude restaurant. Not wanting to repeat the confusion of our first cab experience, we had the hostel innkeeper write the name of the Quanjude restaurant on a business card as well as mark its location on a guest map. It was only a half-mile away! And we had directions! This would be a synch... or so we thought.

Greeted first by a shirtless grandfather triumphantly holding his grandchild, Connor and I followed the twisting pathway from the *Hutongs* into the major roads leading to Tiananmen Square. Once we thought we were in the vicinity of the restaurant, we searched every building in sight within the "never-ending Chinatown." It was as if we were being knocked around in a pinball machine, without a clue as to where our destination was.

Everything was in Chinese, and everyone around us *only* spoke Chinese. Trying to match the curvy symbols of the restaurant name to the huge signs displayed on buildings proved to be, in a word, ineffectual.

After an hour of searching consecutive buildings on three different main streets, we finally found an establishment that appeared to be a restaurant. I handed over the piece of paper to the hostess to confirm that it was the acclaimed Quanjude restaurant. She handed back the paper, giggled, shook her head side-to-side, and pointed down the street. The short-lived relief transformed into a deeper frustration. I rasped, "Anybody speak English?"

She responded, "Nur." At this point, at least five more Chinese employees surrounded us, observing our every move, sizing us up, laughing, and conversing with one another. It felt like we were two show dogs at a best in show. One of the employees grabbed two menus, and motioned for Connor and I to sit at their restaurant.

Although we were still hungry, it was already 8pm, and, on top of that, the restaurant had an A rating (each restaurant in China had a mandated ranking for cleanliness and quality of food), Connor and I responded, "Non Xièxie." We were set in our plans to get to our destination and sink our teeth into the Quanjude Peking Roast Duck.

Back to the search, we began to walk in the direction that the hostess set us on. After four blocks, we arrived at a large black restaurant displaying gaudy red symbols. Parked in front were several black Audis. Connor, who had done quite a bit of research on China, cautioned me that the Audi was the vehicle of choice for the Chinese mafia. Entering the dimly lit dining area, I saw two tables full of suited Chinese men eyeing us. I quickly handed the hostess the paper with the Quanjude Peking Roast Duck name. She immediately shook her head, conversed with another hostess, and gestured some turns down the road. Flummoxed in disbelief, we walked back outside.

Following the hostess's direction, we found a brightly lit restaurant. Connor said with a sigh of relief, "This has to be the place." A smiling hostess welcomed us and began motioning us to a table when I showed her the paper. She giggled, turned to us, and shook her head. We both laughed in amazement. We didn't have the slightest clue how difficult it would be to get to a restaurant. Not to mention, the hostel keepers specially mapped it out – what more could we ask for? We were so hungry and tired that we were more than willing to *screw the duck* and grab a table.

But, Connor and I knew that this was our one chance to visit the *1000 Places* site due to our extensive checklist. Both persistent and unwilling to accept anything less than the Quanjude Peking Roast Duck, we walked out in search of a cab and hoped the driver would understand our directions.

With no cabs in sight, we walked another five city blocks, surrounded by gigantic signs lit in neon Chinese symbols. Sighting another restaurant,

Connor and I walked in and hoped for the best. The lady shook her head, pointed in the direction from where we started, and began giggling uncontrollably while staring us both up and down. A couple servers and hosts walked over, exchanged some words with her, and joined in the laughter.

"Unbelievable," I said to myself. Looking at Connor, I could sense that he felt the same way I did: confused, *yet amused* – what was the big joke? Perturbed from the language disconnect, we darted out and hailed a taxi.

Believe it or not, despite taking many twists and turns, the cab took only ten-minutes to get to the restaurant. Before exiting the cab, I confirmed our location by showing the paper again to the cab driver. He nodded his head. We walked up to a huge building with bright red Chinese symbols and an English translation underneath "Quanjude Peking Roast Duck Restaurant." How gratifying! As we walked inside, a hostess in traditional Chinese garb directed us to an elevator that took us up to the large dining area.

We seated ourselves, removed our backpacks, and had to laugh. The unexpected effort it took to have a simple dinner just blocks away from the hostel was a true test in patience. As we studied the menu, a chef, masterfully slicing the roast duck in the traditional Yuan dynasty fashion, was serving a nearby table. We were starving and grateful to finally enjoy the roast duck of our *hunt*.

We were ready to feast. A journey of uncertainty had eclipsed into an overwhelming feeling of satisfaction. We savored the moment while waiting for the culinary artist to arrive.

The chef made his way over to us, wearing a mouth mask. He began by shaving off the crisp skin of the duck. He then placed hot tea and bowls of broccoli, along with an assortment of vegetables on the table. The skin was part of a Chinese specialty, and dipping it into a sweet sauce made it a masterpiece.

The chef then served the Peking duck onto two plates that Connor and I met with tremendous gratitude. He took a bow of respect and wheeled his cart away, upon which we exclaimed, "Xièxie!"

The meat sizzled, releasing a unique fruity aroma into the air. I asked Connor with excitement, "Are you ready for this?"

Connor chuckled with delight and responded, "Undoubtedly."

We were ready. Our stomachs were growling. We ceremoniously lifted our plastic chopsticks, snagged a slice of tender duck, and placed it into our tongues.

Connor's face was unforgettable. What we thought was going to be a welcoming culinary comfort quickly turned into a cultural shock. Our high expectation for this traditional dish was instantaneously dashed.

We were eating fatty gobs of meat, like uncooked bacon. Flabbergasted, we sampled the vegetables, hoping that it might satiate our hunger. The steamed vegetables were slightly better. Though, the taste was contaminated by that Beijing stench that we first encountered in the *Hutongs*.

Hoping again that the fabled duck skin may be somewhat more palatable, Connor smothered his piece in the special sauce and lifted it to his mouth. I did the same and allowed the duck skin to melt in my mouth. The taste was even worse than the meat! We forced ourselves to try a second bite of the duck, took a couple pictures of the table, and left the

Quanjude restaurant, with empty stomachs and a general feeling of being let down.

Cultural shock crept in, hitting the hardest with the first bite of the Quanjude duck. Walking back through the streets of stench illuminated by Chinese symbols all the way to our mats in the *Hutongs*, the reality had set in.

We thought about cutting the trip short. Meals of fatty meats and dirty vegetables were not appealing in the least. But we knew that there were going to be challenges because we were in a developing region. We decided not to make any changes to our plans. This was China, and we were going to deal with it on our own terms, using any adversity we faced to make us better.

While the dinner didn't come close to meeting my expectations, the night was far from hopeless. Although the meal wasn't exactly enjoyable, it was a unique experience to eat a dish that was enjoyed thousands of years ago by dynasty emperors. Moreover, the start of this trip was a perfect example of the tenacity that it will take to differentiate your unforgettable study abroad journey from a simple memory.

The lesson of the night was to *never settle for mediocrity*. We could have taken the easier option of settling for the first, second, third, or fourth restaurant in order to avoid all the aggravation.

But, we didn't. We were going to have the Quanjude Peking Roast Duck in *1000 Places to See Before You Die*. Period. There was nothing that was going to stop us (unless the Hong Kong mafia came after us). No matter how hungry we were, no matter how late it was, and no matter how aggravating the trip became, we would persevere for the rest of the journey. And that is the mentality that can breed a trip of a lifetime.

––––––––––

You're in the top 1%... Now act like it!

I've had students ask for one piece of advice in getting the most out of their study abroad experience. My answer goes like this: "You are part of the mere one percent of American college students that have the opportunity to study overseas. Putting that in a global perspective, you have the chance to experience something that the supermajority of the world doesn't. Once you've acknowledged this fact, realize that you are truly fortunate and should do *everything* you can to maximize this invaluable experience."

One memory that has always lingered with me took place in Luxor, Egypt. While waiting for a 15-hour train back to Cairo, an Egyptian in his early twenties approached me and asked whether Connor and I were Americans. We said yes.

He responded, "It is my dream to live in America." Teary eyed, he concluded, "It's my life's goal."

We were at a loss for words, never having completely understood how fortunate we were. The young man was right. If he were to migrate to the US, his children and their children would be forever grateful to him for giving them a life in a country based on life, liberty, and the pursuit of happiness. The encounter really bolstered our American patriotism, appreciation for our ancestral immigrants, and ultimately fueled a determination to take studying abroad to the limit.

During the course of studying abroad, you will likely strengthen your appreciation for living in a democratized society. From the 24-hour convenient stores to the accessibility of drinkable water, these luxuries will likely never again be taken for granted. By the end of your study abroad travels, this idea will become clearer than ever.

I can't stress how important it is to realize this at the outset of your trip rather than discover it at the end. Be mindful throughout your travels of this privilege. I promise that it will inject a passion that will help remind you to truly maximize your experience.

In short, it is astounding to travel in another country and have a native let you know of how fortunate you really are. It reminds us to be more appreciative everyday. So, once you have counted your blessings and understood the reality of this great opportunity, expand your horizons to make the most of it. Carpe diem. Do it for your peers. Do it for your family. And, most importantly, *do it for you.*

Simply... Stay positive

This is the best piece of information I can give you in this book. Stay positive. Rhonda Byrne's theme in *The Secret* isn't to be taken lightly. This is such a simple notion -- but it is so easily dismissed due to the aggravations inherent in traveling. The trick to this theory is knowing how to control your attitude. Attitude is everything. You can be mired in a dire situation and rise above it. Be a positive force, avoid temper tantrums, and you will reap positive results.

There were many situations where this mindset allowed Connor and I to achieve our travel goals.

Egypt, again, was the setting. The week before we left, there was a bombing in a Cairo marketplace by a terrorist group targeting tourists. Not surprisingly, Connor, the other twenty-three students, and I were recommended by the school to cancel the trip. Perhaps taking an unnecessary risk, we decided to stick with our plans (I soon found out that explaining it to my parents would be a challenge). There were so many marketplaces in Cairo, so what were the chances? And how could we pass up the Great Pyramids, thousand-year-old mummies, camel trips, and extravagant temples.

Once we arrived in Cairo, the innkeeper reminded us about Luxor, otherwise known as ancient Thebes, which contained the Valley of the Kings and the Temple of Amon-Ra. Getting there required a fifteen-hour train ride, giving us just enough time for a daytrip before returning to Cairo for the flight back to Rome. It was surely a thrilling excursion but risky in terms of timing. Topping that was the fact that thieves regularly target tourists on Egyptian trains.

After weighing the pros and cons, we decided to accept the challenge. We had always planned to see Luxor and couldn't pass up the opportunity. Although there were some discomforts, we were resolute to live in the moment and stay positive through everything. All in all, we were the only two students out of the twenty-five who went to Luxor. Nobody else wanted to deal with the aggravation of twenty hours on a stuffy train. After the fact, many students were bitter about the missed opportunity. It turned out to be the one of the most thrilling experiences in Egypt. The Luxor Temple from 1350 B.C., the Temple of Karnak (the largest temple in the world), intact mummies, and the tombs of pharaohs dug into mountains made Luxor the capital of Egypt's ancient history.

If we did not stay adamant in our plans and had taken the comfortable path, we would not have been on that fifteen-hour train ride to Luxor. Yes, we had to deal with the thirty hours cramped in a diesel train (not to mention being shoulder-to-shoulder with a loudly snoring native). On the way there, we also awoke to French passengers yelling because they were robbed.

We traveled throughout Luxor with a delirium from lack of sleep, but it was all very much worth it. Luxor was in our crosshairs in Egypt, and we weren't going to let any of these obstacles dissuade us. Simply put, being positive and staying on path is crucial to ensure a study abroad experience that you will never forget.

Another example of perseverance was the Scavi tour at the Vatican. My great-uncle, Dr. Roger O'Bryan, who has a true passion for history, informed me of his wish to visit the Vatican Necropolis, also known as the Scavi, which contains the tomb of Peter the Apostle. Located five to twelve meters under Saint Peter's Basilica, Scavi contains hundreds of tombs dating back to the Roman Empire.

The opportunity sounded out of this world. Being a Catholic, I couldn't imagine a greater opportunity. But my high hopes were dimmed when Uncle Roger alerted me that tours were so popular that they had to be booked six to eight months in advance. The Scavi tour allowed no more than twelve people at a time on a guided tour. He recommended that I go to the Vatican Scavi office in the morning to try to join a tour. Wishful thinking, but worth a shot, I thought. Thrilled about the opportunity, I told Connor that we would visit the Vatican the next morning.

After following the directions of a couple Swiss guards, Connor and I met with a man who asked if we had a reservation. I told him no, and he said that there was absolutely no way we could get a tour.

Unwilling to accept no for an answer, we asked if we could go into the office to talk to an official. With a smirk, he pointed us to the Scavi office.

Pushing open the office door, a loud, dramatic Italian fellow appeared at a table and interrogated us, "Scavi? Name!"

I responded, "We have no reservations," looked at Connor and continued, "and were wondering if we could join a tour today."

He started laughing and shook his head, saying, "Do you know how many people are in line for this?" He pulled out a stack of papers about a foot high, and said, "This many!"

Connor explained that we were Loyola students and had just recently learned of the tour. He answered, "Mi dispiace." I was prepared for this answer and knew we had taken it as far as possible in our questioning. So it was time to leave.

As we were about to walk out, the official chimed in, "Okay, okay. You made perfect time for an English tour that is about to start. Fifteen Euros a piece."

We couldn't believe our ears. We were about to pass hundreds of people on a list all because we followed my uncle's suggestion to merely show up and ask. Filled with excitement, we responded, "Molto grazie!" And it turned out to be an unforgettable day in Rome.

We knew that it was just another testament to attaining your goal when one stays optimistic and persistent in their travels. The examples in Luxor and Rome were just two out of a handful we experienced while studying abroad. These opportunities further confirmed how important it is to always keep a positive outlook – this will take you over and beyond your greatest expectations.

Don't be afraid to step outside your comfort zone. Challenge yourself. Stay on track with your set goals. Be prepared to adapt. And I guarantee that you'll enhance your study abroad experience tenfold.

The Bucket List

An extremely useful and practical piece of advice that I can give you is to map out your journey. MAKE A BUCKET LIST.

Bucket List / BUCK-it LIST / *noun*;
1. List containing all of the restaurants, sites, activities, (fill in the blank) that you would like to accomplish before you "kick the bucket" of your study abroad trip.

I cannot tell you how important it is to get down all of your objectives in each city before arriving there. Research each site to figure out which are the most worthwhile to see. Make sure they are reasonable in terms of expenses and your timeframe in the city. Arrange the items by priority just in case you encounter a time conflict and must scrap one. A Bucket List in Europe and China gave us a concrete plan to get away from the haphazardness of the day, and ensure the completion of certain goals. A Bucket List will also give you another avenue to internalize your objectives, and to stay on target for getting them done. Connor and I posted a calendar with must-see sites to constantly remind us of our specific plans.

"Go Forth and Set the World On Fire"

Now that you have prepared a Bucket List, follow St. Loyola's words, and go forth and set the world on fire (not to be mistaken with Nero's example). Don't let your study abroad opportunity slip through your fingers and become *just* a vacation. Test yourself. Don't be afraid to take risks. Don't jump on the bandwagon. Be unique and accomplish what you desire... Getting out of your comfort zone is how you grow not only as a traveler, but also as a *person*.

Don't allow setbacks to slow you down. You control the speedometer of your travels. It is your own perspective that dictates your experiences abroad... actually your entire life. Yes, you are in control of the entirety of your trip. Are you going to make the day trip that you've been excited about even though your friends want to relax at campus for the day? Will plans fall through when you find that your itinerary involves much more work than anticipated? Will you forgo the night out with friends to see your planned Trevi Fountain under the stars? There are hundreds of choices to be made. And they are all for *you* to make. You are in a position that only one percent of students ever experience. Stay in motion, don't dwell in mediocrity, and take the road less traveled. Success will find you abroad.

Study Abroad Bucket List

11. Finding Faith in Studying Abroad

Discovering Sanctity at the Holy Stairs in Rome, Italy:

Scala Sancta is Italian for "Holy Stairs." The Holy Stairs are twenty-eight white marble steps, now encased in wood and located in the old Lateran palace. Their significance stems from the fact that they originally led to Pontius Pilate's house in

Jerusalem. More specifically, they were the very steps that Jesus Christ walked on his way to trial. For centuries, Christians have venerated the Passion of Jesus by walking up the wooden stairway on their hands and knees and saying a prayer for each step. In 1511, Martin Luther experienced a turning point in his life when ascending the stairway. These stairs are a fixture for any serious pilgrim's list.

When my Uncle Roger informed me of this opportunity, I knew that it was a must-see item on the Bucket List. Along with the prospect of adventure in studying abroad came the spectra of a religious experience. It's no secret that Rome is the hub of the Roman Catholic Church. For me, Rome opened endless opportunities to deepening my faith, reliving its history, and delving into mysteries underlying the Catholic faith ~ something that 20th Century authors Flannery O'Connor and Graham Greene refer to as the *Catholic imagination.* You may be thinking to yourself: what could that term possibly mean? There isn't much imagination to Catholic ceremonies that have repeated the same old customs for the last two millennia! Like you, the term didn't make much sense to me until a literature class at Loyola University Chicago. Father Mark Bosco referred to the *Catholic Imagination* as the life of sacramentality and paradox. It is the very manifestation that affirms the Church's belief system in the sacraments and mystery of the Father, Son, and Holy Spirit. The *Catholic imagination* seemed like it was present in every corner and crevasse of Rome. It mysteriously lies within the history and atmosphere of the ancient city.

The Holy Stairs sounded like the perfect way to experience a part of Rome's *Catholic Imagination*. I was drawn to the life of the stairway and its sacred significance in hopes to discover meditation, open-mindedness, and faith while studying abroad...

It was a rainy day in Rome. I was used to the usual rainfall in March by then. The local Italians would say, "Marzo è pazzarello," translated into "March is crazy." The rainy landscape along with the overflowing fountains at St. Peter's Square is a very picturesque scene. I obtained a map of Rome to lead us to the location of the Holy Stairs.

This was unlike any other adventure in Rome. It was a long trip with multiple bus transfers, all the while not knowing exactly where to get off. Connor and I were simultaneously scrutinizing side streets in search of the Lateran Palace, containing the Holy Stairs. Drenched from the weather, we finally came across the robust Basilica of Saint John Lateran, which was directly across the street from the Lateran Palace.

As Connor and I threw open the giant ancient doorway to the Lateran Palace, I peered up the wooden stairway to see three nuns whispering the Hail Mary while clenching their rosaries. The silence was so consuming that I immediately sensed that we, indeed, were in a sacred place.

As we walked inside, a silence revoked the calamity of the noisy Roman streetcars. Candles illuminated the room, showcasing the intricacy of exquisite 13th century frescoes on the ceiling of the Holy Stairs. Beyond the stairway was a small chapel, the Holy of Holies, used as a personal chapel by the early Popes in the Lateran Palace. I clasped my hands in a reverent manner as I lowered my knees to the wooden encasement of the stairway.

When I placed my knees on the stairway and lowered my head, I envisioned that biblical event of the Passion of Jesus that set stage on the stairway. Closing my eyes, I saw Pontius Pilate exclaiming to the Jews after having Jesus scourged, "Behold, your King!" Once Jesus had mounted the steps, the crowds shouted acrimoniously, "Take him away! Take him away! Crucify him!" The scene had replayed in my head over and over again before, but this time, it had become much more vivid. It was tough to comprehend that these were the actual steps from Jerusalem where Jesus was convicted. I muttered a prayer before shifting my weight onto step two.

I didn't get the full experience of the Holy Stairs until I took my second step. As I shifted my weight from my left to right leg onto the next step, a sudden pain shot up into both thighs. My tibia bone met the hard and uneven wood with a jolting pain. As I attempted to balance myself, I looked at Connor who smiled with me at the unpredictability of it all. I have to admit that it was quite tempting to shortcut a prayer to finish up the assent as quickly as possible. But I didn't want to diminish the experience so I dismissed the easy out and said a prayer.

Using my hands to help leverage my weight to the next step, my knees met the wood, again with jolting pain. I began to wonder, "How is this that painful for me and it seemed like a synch for the nuns!" After another step, I rebalanced, ignored the knee pain, and tried to meditate into prayer. I winced, "Only twenty-four steps to go!" I began to notice at the fifth step that my legs began to actually quiver from the digging of my kneecaps into the hard wood.

I slowly raised my head again, not to look at Connor, but to the top of the Holy Stairs... Then, it hit me. At the very top of the stairway on the back wall, overlooking the pilgrims, was a Renaissance fresco of Mary and John at the foot of the cross. The artist painted the fresco in such a way that Jesus's face clearly depicted His suffering to those who saw it. The Catholic Imagination came to me at that moment.

My knee pain suddenly evaporated. The paradoxical nature of the circumstances became apparent. I thought to myself, the Catholic Imagination at its finest. The pain that Jesus endured on the cross had no comparison to ascending the wooden steps on my hands and knees. It was a fulfilling feeling. It was my first real experience of Rome's Catholic Imagination at work. Not just some wooden art spelling out a story, it was a ritual that enlightened its visitors, uniquely connecting themselves to its message. The paradox between the pilgrims' and Jesus's pain was clear. As I continued to crawl the steps and say prayers, Jesus's insurmountable sacrifice became progressively surreal to me.

At the twenty-eighth step, Connor and I quickly jumped to our feet after saying our last prayer. It was a powerful experience that I couldn't have imagined missing. In a meditative perspective, it taught its visitors to reach their inner peace in the midst of their physical pain. I couldn't have imagined a better opportunity to find the mystery of the Catholic Imagination in Rome. With legs like metal stints, I walked into a small gift shop ran by the nuns where I bought a mini portrait of Saint Padre Pio, as a reminder of the invaluable lesson that I learned that day.

Make the Leap!

"Have no fear of moving into the unknown. Simply step out fearlessly knowing that I am with you, therefore no harm can befall you; all is very, very well. Do this in complete faith and confidence."
~Pope John Paul II.

Delving into the unknown is most likely the crux of your decision to study abroad. You want to get out of your comfort zone and explore the world! There are so many exhilarating experiences to be had and countless inspiring places waiting for you. This may sound simple to pursue, but your natural proclivity for comfort will repeatedly jump in your way. Dealing with the uncertainty and discomfort of experiencing a new world without the luxury of your family, group of friends, easy access to your iPhone, iPad, or MacBook will inevitably threaten your pursuit to make the most of your study abroad experience.

These factors may not specifically affect you in the slightest way, but you would be surprised by the struggle that students face in the adjustment abroad. Some become so intensely frustrated that they fly home. Students deal with the adjustment to the unknown in a variety of ways: some unhealthy and counterproductive, such as excessive drinking or drug use, while others engage in a familiar pastime, such as reading, writing, exercising, or converging with a close friend. Pope John Paul II's remark reminds us that, regardless of how you may deal with the unknown, the constant is faith.

Whatever your religion, faith is inherent in studying abroad. You can *and should* attain a deeper understanding of your own faith while studying overseas. Listening to the chiming bells of Notre Dame, smelling the strong Frankincense Resin scent burning in St. Peter's Basilica, feeling the grainy sand of the Sahara Desert, awing at the perfect half sphere of the Pantheon, and meditating at dusk on the Spanish Steps when there's not a tourist in sight – all will take you there. A moment of silence can bring you deeper into your faith. I guarantee that it will make all the difference...

While building a renewed appreciation of your faith, you will find a deeper meaning to your study abroad adventures. It will become not only be a trip a trip to see the world, but also a pilgrimage in itself. In turn, your faith will give you the strength to delve further into the unknown. Consequently, and most notably, you will move further from your comfort zone and discover yourself outwardly growing as a person. *This is often said to be the ultimate goal of studying abroad.* You will surprisingly find that the more uncomfortable of a position that you find yourself in, the clearer your own sense of *self* becomes. Now that you have read about the opportunities of studying abroad, make the leap of faith and, in Pope John Paul II's words, "have no fear of moving into the unknown."

Find a Spot to Meditate and Do it!

You may or may not be a fan of meditation. It may not strike you as a useful or exciting pastime, but I assure you, it will be productive in your time studying abroad. I am not telling you to become a devotee of Confucius by any means, but spending some time throughout your travels will help keep you on target with your plans. Once you have recollected your experiences abroad in a reflective setting, you will want to make it part of your agenda because it is so relaxing and useful. It allows you to jump off the bustling path... take a step back... and examine your set goals. Internalize your experiences ~ and appreciate the opportunities awaiting you. Now I will share three examples of experiences I found to be effective for achieving this heightened state of peace and gratitude.

One that I will always remember was in Istanbul, Turkey. We had taken a ferry down the Riva River to the city of Çayağzı, which to my surprise was apart of Asia. Waiting for us was an aged stony fortress, grilled fish sandwiches sold by natives off the harbor, hilly grasslands, and a picturesque view of the Black Sea. We were told to be back in three hours ~ so we had some time to kill.

Connor and I each picked a grassy patch so we could sit, reflect, and meditate. I spent forty-five minutes thinking about how blessed I was to be there while admiring the beauty of the Black Sea. It also allowed me time to examine myself in terms of whether I was meeting my set goals. Specifically, I thought about my developing perspective of the world while gaining a deeper appreciation of faith. That became my most prized memory of that trip because of its serenity and time for reflection.

Another memorable meditation was in Beijing, China, during the ten kilometers hike on the Great Wall. Connor and I were told to choose the Simatai site, located seventy-five miles north of Beijing, because it is one of the few sites to retain the original features of the Ming Dynasty Great Wall. I had also remembered that UNESCO designated the Simatai site as one of the World Culture Heritage Sites. The place is known for its thirty-five beacon towers and its rough terrain, which made the experience all the more surreal. We decided that Simatai was a must.

The view was incredible: the battle wall sprawled for miles upon miles, scaling up and down mammoth, green mountains. Simatai was definitely living up to its designation as a Great Wonder of the World. After we escaped the local farmers pedaling trinkets during the hike, we took a silent moment to enjoy the spectacular view. I sat on a large mortar stone and pictured what it would have been like during the Mongol raids in the 14th Century.

Once outside the hustle and bustle of Beijing, I gained a whole new perspective of China. The silence of the present moment, and awe-inspiring structure of the past presented the perfect opportunity to think. Just taking the time to inhale the Miyun air, savoring the serenity, and imagining the ancient history of the Wall was very enlightening. In total, the silence and age of the Simatai site made it a very worthwhile and spiritually fulfilling stop in China.

The last meditation experience I'd like to share with you was in Fu Xing Park of the French Concession in Shanghai. While walking around the lake, I was surprised to discover an eighty-year-old local man lifting himself by his toes and dropping repeatedly. Connor and I looked at each other, wondering what this man could possibly be doing. Once I looked in the Fodor's travel book under Fu Xing Park, I quickly discovered that the park was a haven for *tai chi*, a type of Chinese martial arts from the 16th century. It was particularly common among the elderly because it was said to promote longevity. As I walked closer to the center of the park, I saw groups of locals slowly moving their arms in circular, controlled motions while softly twisting their hips. We were awed not only by the sheer number of locals that participated in *tai chi*, but also by their sense of calmness and agility.

I had to jump into a group of five natives and experience this for myself. At first, I was very careful in my motions, trying to be respectful, as to not offend their unique art. But once I came closer, I laughed to myself at the very thought of asking permission to join in their circle. Fortunately, the natives were some of the most welcoming people in the world. I was a bit surprised when an old woman, while leading a small group, smiled and motioned for me stand in front ~ right next to her. In five minutes, I felt like one of the locals, mirroring the leader's every move. Losing Old Town's tourist traps and acquiring one-on-one interaction with Shanghai natives was priceless to me. It gave me the chance to learn *tai chi* movements, or as I like to call it *meditation in motion*, while exploring the harmony and peacefulness embedded in that ancient Chinese picture.

A meditation experience can be invaluable. Whether it is brought about by interaction with the locals, internalizing the beauty of one's surroundings, or through a spiritual examination of yourself ~ it will add *more* to your study abroad experience. The Dalai Lama said in his Instructions for Life mantra, "Remember that silence is sometimes the best answer." His words especially ring true when you take the time for yourself to sit down, breathe deeply, and allow your imagination to explore the hidden origins inherent in your adventures. There will be plenty of time for joking with friends and listening to tour guides, but make time for meditation and reflection. I guarantee that it will bring a fulfilling, special meaning to your trips, as they have with mine.

Don't Sell Yourself Short

Even though you may not be "religious", spirituality permeates our lives. Don't blindly follow the crowd of study abroad students who don't take the time to make something more of their study abroad trip. Studying abroad isn't only about seeing great new places. It is also food for the soul. The whole idea of studying overseas is to push yourself outside the box and find *you*. Don't fall into the quagmire that envelopes some unfortunate students with too big an ego to recognize the great opportunity and lose out on the spiritual side of the travel. Simply put, *don't sell yourself short*.

As a student, this is likely the greatest opportunity you'll have for self-improvement. Make your study abroad experience a spiritual journey ~ your own spiritual metamorphism to grow closer to God, to your spirit, or to both. The worst mistake that you can make while studying abroad is to ignore these opportunities. You are about to explore a different culture, and with that, a multitude of religions, traditions, and idealisms. Be open to your own spiritual life. Being open to your spiritual life doesn't necessarily mean to go to a place of worship. It means taking the time to listen to yourself for a part of the day, or taking a walk around the campus abroad to enjoy the outdoors. Let go of your everyday stress and nurture your own *self*.

During the course of your travels, you will cross paths with the Islamic, Roman Catholic, Jewish, and Protestant religions. Don't be afraid to explore other religions just because they are different than your own. Learning about other religions will help deepen your understanding of a city's history. For example, Rome was largely shaped by the presence of the Roman Catholic Church. Walking into the Blue Mosque of Istanbul, the Parthenon of Athens, or St. Paul Outside the Wall of Rome can be an overwhelmingly spiritual experience for anyone. You can't help but appreciate the masterful architecture and ornate artwork ~ all inspired by faith. Be open to finding this connection with yourself and others. You will absorb the significance of your destinations and experience each one to the absolute *fullest*.

The Three Reflections
1) If travelling to northern Italy, make sure to stop in the most medieval city in the world, San Gimignano. At a distance, one will find the fourteen daunting medieval towers standing together in the small city.

Walking into San Gimignano at dusk, you can catch the scent of burning oak amidst the starlit sky, and walk through the city's dark, winding tunnels. It was definitely "a catching city," just as my mother had put it. Experiencing this surreal scene gave me such an appreciation for Italian culture. Smelling the burning oak and wandering through this enchanted citadel was like being in a King Arthur storybook. While enjoying the mystery of the city, I was so grateful for the opportunity I had. The experience really gave me insight into the remarkable settings that we were blessed with on Earth.

2) On the train from X'ian to Shanghai, a couple asked Connor and I to hold their two young children for a picture. The two children made a peace sign, and were genuinely thrilled to get a picture with these two unusually tall Americans. I couldn't believe how open Chinese people were, just giving strangers their children for a picture. You would never see this in America. The experience really made an impression on me because of their kindheartedness. They were genuinely happy individuals who showed us respect, and gave me a perspective of how people should really treat each other.

3) Walking into the first Jesuit Church in Rome, the Gesù, also known as the Church of the Most Sacred

Name of Jesus, was truly inspiring. The Gesù holds the tomb of the Jesuit order's founder, St. Ignatius of Loyola, and a relic of his assistant, Francis Xavier; his arm encased within a glass reliquary. As I walked into the Church, I peered at the rooms where St. Ignatius lived for twelve years and envisioned him working tirelessly on his manuscripts. I could sense the holiness of the Church, and was awestruck being in the presence of St. Ignatius. Being a student of Loyola University Chicago, I couldn't be more ecstatic with the setting. I said a prayer and walked around, marveling at the ceiling artwork, overflowing in its Renaissance mastery. I thought that the beautiful interior of the Church was an appropriate fit for the tomb of St. Ignatius. My experience, consisting of both beautiful works and deep thought, became a very significant moment for me in Rome.

These three experiences brought profound meaning and significance to my study abroad. Being open to spirituality will make a world of difference for your travels. Taking the time to meditate or reflecting on yourself will bring you closer to the *Truth*. The time spent will be some of the most worthwhile moments during your time abroad. If done right, your adventures will surely be more productive and, unsurprisingly, much more memorable.

12. Avoid the Eurotrip at all Costs

"Al Dolce Vita" in Sienna, Italy:

The time was January 10, 2008. The place was
Sienna, Italy. The John Felice Rome Center began its
study abroad program with an orientation in Sienna
at a hilltop hotel, overlooking some of Italy's fine
vineyards. We ate a dinner consisting of house wine,

bread loaves, and *Rigatoni All'Amatriciana*, and listened to the welcoming speech. Afterwards, Connor and I decided to take a stroll around the hotel. We searched the premises and found the hotel "BAR."

It was your average type of hotel bar with the *barristo* in the back wiping the counters ~ still sticky from limoncello the night before. There was no one there besides a few campus administrators. The other students were already out in search of Sienna's bustling nightlife. Once we sat down at the bar, the *barristo*, who looked like *Igor* from the film *Young Frankenstein*, smiled and said, "Ciao, dimi."

We responded, "Ciao," and tried to pull off some *Italiano* but were unsuccessful in our attempts since we hadn't even started learning the language.

The *barristo* chuckled and said, wiping the inside of a martini glass, "What can I get for you?" I was instantly relieved that one of the first Italians we met were friendly in spite of our lack of *Italiano*.

I replied, "What would you recommend for an authentic Italian drink?" He lowered his head in thought and scratched his weathered black hair for a minute with his rough *barristo* hands that had mixed, poured, and muddled drinks for ages.

He lifted his head with a child's giddiness and answered boldly with one finger raised, "A café extra!"

"What is a café extra," you might ask. That is what Connor and I thought as we confusedly looked at each other, expecting the answer to be *limoncello* or *sassolino*. The *barristo* popped open an aged bottle of grappa, and poured three shots in separate martini glasses. I knew that he was a good *barristo* then and there because a true *barristo* would lead by example! Next, he turned on the espresso machine, placed fresh ground coffee into its basket, and waited for the hot delight to flow out of the reservoir. Once the espressos were prepared, he poured each one into the martini glasses while mixing the grappa and espresso together.

The *barristo* slid two glasses in our direction, and kept one for himself, saying "*Buon Appetito.*" The drinks were far from an alcoholic drink that I would typically enjoy. But who could pass up such a unique Italian specialty recommended by a *barristo* veteran? We all lifted our glasses, and the *barristo* was the first to speak. "*Al dolce vita.*" The translation is "To life." We responded accordingly and tossed it back. And wow, it tasted just as awful as it sounded. It was definitely a *barristo's* acquired taste! We both gave him a *"grazie"* for a shot that we would never forget.

Connor asked the *barristo* where we could find a unique pub in the city, and he referred us on a map to the *Barone Rosso* bar, smack dab in the middle of the city. He ordered us to take another café extra if we were going out on the town. We respectfully declined the offer but accepted to take a shot of grappa with this most cordial of men.

We walked down the hotel entrance path in the brisk night air, excited about the beginning of our study abroad journey. We laughed at the thought of how that *barristo* could have actually enjoyed the café extra. We knew that it was the first of many cultural surprises we would discover. Arriving at the *Barone Rosso*, we saw that the Rome Center students were already enjoying themselves and getting to know each other. We got our drinks, and Connor and I relived our learnt words from the *barristo*, "Al dolce vita." Everyone responded, "Al dolce vita."

Connor and I ordered a couple other drinks that night, but nothing close to the famed "café extra." It was a really fun night, and a great way to start off our adventure while getting to know other students. The next morning, all of the students' appearances were anything but inconspicuous. One of the program's administrators asked us in amusement, "Were you guys being good last night?"

The boozing and partying in Sienna was enjoyable, and back home it was somewhat normal for college students. But it wasn't something that Connor and I planned on consistently doing during the course of studying overseas.

––––––––––

Monitor Your Partying

Before I begin giving you snippets of advice, I'd like to make a disclaimer. I am not here to be a parent. I am not here to dictate how to spend your time abroad. I am here to impart to you the things that I have learned along the way – as well as the things that I wish I had known before boarding the plane to Rome. And one of the bits of advice I feel is imperative if you're going to have the best experience abroad is this: *Avoid the hard partying Eurotrip.* That being said, let me begin.

The majority of students don't realize until later on how foolish it is to make their study abroad program a "party away from home." This is a huge issue for every student studying abroad. Students abroad will drink day and night, and I don't mean enjoying a couple glasses of red wine at a Roman *enoteca* or perhaps a café extra at lunch. I literally mean drink like a fish within the confines of the student dormitory and reenact "Woodstock" almost every day. It isn't surprising that putting a huge group of college students in a campus far away would produce such results.

It has been such an issue abroad that I have witnessed campuses taking disciplinary action against study abroad students for drug use and other disorderly behavior. Unbelievable isn't it? You are investing thousands and thousands of dollars to presumably gain an entirely new perspective of the world outside of your own. The fact that schools must enjoin disciplinary action against inappropriate behavior is a testament to the unfortunate decisions that routinely take place. Reverting to that sort of behavior also questions those students' outlook as to the reason for studying abroad. The fact that you are reading this book, striving to make the most out of your experience, leads me to believe that it won't be an issue.

However, I don't intend to say that you should never party while studying abroad. There's no reason why you shouldn't have a good time out with friends once in a while. Indeed, I occasionally partied while abroad with friends, starting at campus and going out to some bar in Rome. Or you may choose to experience the nightlife of Athens while in Greece or the tapas bars of Barcelona while in Spain. There is a time and place for everything, and, again, partying isn't per se unacceptable while abroad.

But treating this truly once-in-a-lifetime opportunity as a Eurotrip will undoubtedly minimize or cut out valuable experiences to be had. Making it a habit to drink excessively will limit everything abroad, from the ability to 'discover yourself' to the exploration of your must-see sites. So do yourself a huge favor and monitor the amount of partying for just a semester! This time in your life will be over before you know it. Savor it. Explore unseen lands. And don't waste it away on alcohol.

An Unfortunate Reality

I'd like to return to the notion in Chapter eleven that students abroad will commonly fall within the ambits of homesickness, loneliness, or boredom throughout their semester. These, in turn, will sometimes cause students to seek out the easiest way to enjoy their time: drinking and lounging. But every minute you have is invaluable ~ and there is no better way to throw this exciting opportunity in the waste can than for you to constantly join the partying herd. And this won't be a temptation once in a while. The unfortunate reality is that you are likely to encounter these types of issues all the time. So be prepared to stick out like a sore thumb if you want to maximize your time. As I had said before, there is nothing wrong with drinking with friends once in a while. But, when you decide to distance yourself from your fifteen friends who want to have a drinking marathon, you will unfortunately find that you, and perhaps a couple others, will be the odd ones out.

Being hung-over at an 8am tour of the Colosseum or while watching the sunrise stretch along Sicily's Greco-Roman coastline is not what studying abroad is about. It isn't exactly fun for yourself, but, besides that, you won't be able fully appreciate the visit. You are there to immerse yourself in a culture, interact with the natives, get lost in a city, take a whiff of the air, and get as much out of the experience as possible. There is no room for feeling "crappy" when you explore city's treasures. There is not a second to waste, even in all five months. As my great-great-great aunt from Trento, Italy, had once said, "It is impossible to see all of Rome in a lifetime." And that idea lies in every city you see.

So be yourself, and take the road less traveled. The

success of your study abroad adventure is deeply rooted in your ability to stay on track with your plans and not fall into the unfortunate wayside of turning it into a Eurotrip.

The Tradeoff

If you decide to party more often than not, yes, it will be fun. You will have some blurry memories while getting trashed in a foreign country ~ but is that how you want to define your study abroad experience? Are you spending thousands of dollars to party with your friends or to truly experience other cultures and places? It is completely *your* decision to make.

Do you want to search your destination cities to their limits? Well, I can say that Connor and my decision not to party was the pre-determined factor that *truly made our trip*. One particular example is when we woke up early one morning to trail around Rome for hours. Searching its narrow pathways, we came upon an odd building, with windows that were whitewashed as to not reveal the inside. There was no sign outside either, which was very mysterious. As we walked in, there was a sign which read *"Felice a Testaccio."* As I looked towards the center, I saw several tables of locals laughing and conversing over their *carpaccio* dishes. Some gave us the stare down

since we were unknown in the neighborhood.
I suddenly realized that we had found an Italian gem,
stashed away from the taint of tourism. The pasta
and steak dinner was the finest meal I had in Rome.
The fact that we had searched the city and came
upon such an authentic place made the whole
experience that much more special.

Another example was in Shanghai when, after
exploring the city, Connor and I came across Cloud
9. Cloud 9 is a lounge located on the eighty-seventh
floor of the Grand Hyatt Hotel and overlooks the
city's skyline. It had a remarkable view of the
Oriental Pearl Tower, which is a building that will
make you think twice about whether you are still on
this planet or not. As we so often experienced, once
the owners found out we were Americans, they
immediately seated us even though the lounge
seemed to be full. It was remarkable how many times
we were specially treated for that very reason. While
on the eighty-seventh floor, Connor and I conversed
over a cocktail about how grateful we were to find
such a place so different from Beijing. The
appreciation and cultural learning was at an all-time
high.

Another example where exploration of a city paid off
was in Hangzhou, China. Being in China, Connor

and I felt that we had taken a turn for the worst when it came to cuisine. Our daily foods were void of any complete protein. When we found a Subway in Xi'an, China, we felt like a passerby ship had saved our raft... But when we found *Shanhe Teppanyaki* in Hangzhou, we were ecstatic. Located around the city's famous *West Lake*, the restaurant served its guests with on-site chefs that prepared steaks, chicken, and vegetable dishes right in front of you. Connor and I enjoyed filets with charred mushrooms, a variety of mango dishes, and Japanese beer. The Chinese hunger that had existed for the entire trip had begun to fade away. It was indeed a gastronomical find.

These three simple examples demonstrate how we benefitted from choosing not to continuously party and waste time. If Connor and I had decided to party more often, it is unlikely that we would ever have had stumbled onto these unique experiences. Good thing, because each of them taught us new lessons and helped define our study abroad adventure. You can capitalize on your study abroad experience by choosing not to be apart of the Eurotrip and, by doing so, seize as many extraordinary opportunities as possible. Again, it is your decision to make; you are in control.

Take Off – Live in the Moment

Don't be setback by bad choices. This is YOUR time. Make every moment of it count. Be prepared to live on the edge and discover new experiences. Don't be afraid to try something new and exhilarating and perhaps overcome a fear.

Experience the world's highest two hundred and thirty-three meter bungee jump at Macau Tower in South China.

Face your fear of skydiving and free fall from a helicopter at thirteen thousand feet into the mountainous and pristine setting of Interlaken, Switzerland.

Charter your adventure to the Sahara Desert in Tunisia where you will literally be jumping the sand dunes in desert buggies.

Take a Turkish bath in Istanbul, Turkey, to experience the royal treatment of the Ottoman kings.

Create a bucket list and work towards fulfilling that list throughout your journey. Most importantly, *live in the moment*. Savor every minute in your chosen destination in order to fully embrace the experience.

Visit the ancient seaside *medina* in Hammamet, Tunisia, and walk through the Arab *souks* to find a variety of golden plates, baskets of fresh spices, and Middle Eastern fabrics.

Rent a *vespa* in Rome via *Piazza Barberini* with a friend and wiz around the gigantic structure of the Colosseum, the Pantheon, the Vittorio Emanuele Memorial, and the Spanish Steps.

Take the mopeds and stroll through all of the unique parks that Rome has to offer: *Villa Ada, Villa Borghese, Villa Doria Pamphili, and Villa Torlonia.*

Take the time to watch in awe at the beauty of the sunset and rising moon in the Sahara Desert.

Marvel at the human mastery of the Parthenon of Athens from 447 BC, the Great Wall of China from 700 BC, and the Great Pyramid of Giza from 2560 BC.

And, *most importantly*, make sure you put your ALL into every moment. Wherever you end up... go for it! Strive to make memories that will truly last a lifetime. Make it an experience that you will look back to and not regret one minute.

Conclusion (Sean)

I am so glad that you have given me the opportunity to tell you what I know about studying abroad. I hope it helps you maximize your experience. Part of the *Truth* is your memories will become more or less hazy a few years after your study abroad. To fix this, you must remember "to remember." Make it a point to record lots of videos and relive every special moment abroad in the years to come. Our goal is to provide you with the information we wished we had gotten before we lifted off to study overseas (Not just the same old checklist of what to bring and where to visit). We wanted to sketch a more personal and useful picture of what to expect and how to maximize your potential.

The hope Connor and I have is not only to inform you, but also to instill a deep passion in you to make the most of your study abroad journey. There are unparalleled opportunities waiting for you abroad. Be ready to create memories to last a lifetime. If you have any questions or concerns, feel free to email me at obryan.sean@yahoo.com. I look forward to hearing from you.

Best Wishes,
Sean

Conclusion (Connor)

In the subsequent weeks, months, and even years after returning home, you will slowly begin to realize how valuable this experience truly was. Sooner or later the *Truth* will be revealed, and all the situations you encounter back home will suddenly seem a little bit easier than before. **The *Truth* is: you will approach life's challenges with confidence and certainty rather than apprehension and worry because you've faced difficulties abroad head on... and conquered them.** I hope it was and will continue to be a journey of self-discovery that will enhance your life long after you return.

I wish you well my friend, feel free to e-mail me at connor.lavallie@yahoo.com with any questions, comments, concerns, or to simply tell me a little about your experiences abroad. I look forward to hearing from you.

Best regards,
Connor

Appendix A

Tips from real students who've been there and back:

We'd like to think our perspectives have been *everything* you could ever need, and it's helped you become more excited and informed about studying abroad. However I know you may have more questions, and it always helps learn more. Therefore, we decided to conduct some interviews.

We spoke with a wide range of students from different schools all over the world. Each of them has studied abroad for a minimum of one full semester in Europe, China, Australia, New Zealand, and other regions. We asked each of them these four questions:

1) *What do you wish you would have known before you left to study abroad?*
2) *What advice would you give someone if they wanted to really maximize their experience?*
3) *Any useful tips for a student studying abroad today?*
4) *What are some things they should they try to avoid?*

Mariam P. <u>Studied in: Europe</u>

What do you wish you would have known before you left to study abroad?
I guess this is sort of existential, but I wish I had known of my own ability to adapt and be comfortable in a foreign country. Otherwise, I wish I really had done more research on exactly what I wanted to do/see. I feel like I wasted a lot of time at the JFRC [their campus] when I could have been out more.

What advice would you give someone if they wanted to really maximize their experience?
GO OUT and experience your city. Not just the bars or the tourist spots, but really experience it. Force yourself to even use your very limited speaking ability to get around.

Any useful tips for a student studying abroad today?
Try to pick up some of the language before going; it really does open up other windows. Aside from getting to know people at the JFRC better, you get to know the locals and you might even meet some cool students at the English-Language school.

What are some things they should they try to avoid?

Avoid catching cabin fever, and get out of your home-base abroad. If you're complaining about the facilities, you're spending too much time there. GET OUT.

Lys Z. Studied in: Europe

What do you wish you would have known before you left to study abroad?

I guess I wish I would have known how important friends abroad become when you get home. A lot of people back in the states don't quite understand how meaningful being abroad is [if they haven't gone] so it is really nice to have that strong support group.

What advice would you give someone if they wanted to really maximize their experience?

I would say travel to the countries you would not plan on vacationing to later in your life. Explore those places that you have the best access to, and make sure that you spend a ton of time in the city/ country you are studying abroad in as well. A lot of people don't spend enough time in the city they live in and don't truly get to know the culture they are a part of. A few small things: make a budget before you go, never say no to an adventure whether it is a walk through the city, or a trip with people you don't usually hang out with, try to spend a lot of time going out to bars/restaurants not catered to tourists and Americans.

Any useful tips for a student studying abroad today?

I can't stress enough how important it is to make a budget. Don't go anywhere with a huge group of friends. With a smaller group, you are forced to explore more, and move out of your comfort zone. Eat a lot of the food there, take a few days by yourself in your study abroad city... and don't bring a map, just explore what's around you. [I would do this when you have a decent grasp on the area first]

What are some things they should they try to avoid?

Avoid touristy places as much as you can, cliques, spending too much time connecting with people back home [you will miss out on a lot] Avoid getting pick-pocketed by following the suggestions in this book, and safety pinning zippers on your backpack together [it takes to long for them to unfasten, so it's very difficult for thieves to take your things] Don't overspend on souvenirs [pick a few things you know you want to spend money on, and don't buy extras... for me, buying clothes was not an option because I was on a tight budget and wanted to spend my money on travel and adventures]

Kerry L. - <u>Studied in: Europe</u>

What do you wish you would have known before you left to study abroad?

I would have liked to of known more information on what the locals are like, how they dress, act, travel, communicate. I would have almost wanted a crash course in the culture to be a bit more acclimated to the different way of life.

What advice would you give someone if they wanted to really maximize their experience?

To maximize the experience, definitely do not be afraid to travel and use all the time you have. That is one thing that I regret not doing enough of. I spent too much time doing my schoolwork, and not out going into the city and exploring. Bring a map with you, and just roam around and see where you go.

Any useful tips for a student studying abroad today?

Just be brave and go everywhere. Find friends that have the same travel style and you will get more out of the experience. Do not be afraid to splurge on a good meal, wine, museum, and ticket somewhere. Just live up everything the place has to offer. Do as much as you can... anything that the natives do.

What are some things they should they try to avoid?

Avoid getting into arguments with natives. Just be pleasant and respectful, don't fight or cause a scene. You have to remember that although you are temporarily living there, you are a guest in that country.

Bethany D. - Studied in: Europe and Asia

What do you wish you would have known before you left to study abroad?

I wish I would have known more about the people in the places that I went. By that I mean that I wish I had read more novels or other books about the typical life of a person in that country. Also, I wish I would have known more about the government, and how it affects the day-to-day life of the people.

What advice would you give someone if they wanted to really maximize their experience?

I would say that don't limit yourself, and try everything at least once. It you are in China and someone offers you yak butter tea, or fried scorpion on a stick... try it! Don't be afraid to use the language. I sound like a fool when I try to speak Chinese, but the people love it and they try to help me out with learning new words, it creates a kind of bond.

Any useful tips for a student studying abroad today?

Don't be afraid to go big. Going to a country where you don't speak the language shouldn't limit you, it is easy to communicate with people whether it be by pointing at something or trying to act things out. It makes for funny stories too!

What are some things they should they try to avoid?

Try to avoid calling home or being on Facebook all the time. Try not to stay in your clique or group of friends the whole time. Get out and meet new people. Try and make friends from the country that you are in, they know all the best places to go and they will become an invaluable resource.

Amelia B. - <u>Studied in: Europe</u>

What do you wish you would have known before you left to study abroad?

I wish that I would have known that part of the study abroad experience is just letting go and experiencing the place that you are in. You can get so wrapped up in the logistics before you go to Europe, or where ever, that when you get there it seems so surreal for a while. I wish someone would have told me to just take it all in. I also wish someone would have told me to take a journal, and take time each day to jot memorable moments of each day down. It may seem like you have much better things to do while you are there (like explore) rather than journal, but when you come back, you will really like to be able to flip through that amazing memory log and relive all of the amazing things that happened.

What advice would you give someone if they wanted to really maximize their experience?
I would tell them to branch out and meet new people. It's really great to go study abroad with your best friends, but part of the experience is meeting new people and building relationships with others in some of the most amazing places you will ever be. This includes locals. One of my favorite people I met, and became friends with in Europe was an art vendor in Rome ~ I feel like I could go back right now, sit and have an hour long conversation with him.

Any useful tips for a student studying abroad today?
Don't travel so much that you miss out on the place that you are in. Don't forget that the city that you are in has lots to offer and that part of the reason you went there is to see and explore that place. I think there were a lot of people I was with that traveled so much, and then within the last week they were trying

to shove in all these places in our city they never got to see. Make sure you give yourself plenty of time to make your study abroad city your home too.

What are some things they should they try to avoid?

Avoid getting wrapped up in the details. Enjoy getting lost. Put away your map and wander [Do it safely] Avoid the really fancy looking restaurants; the ones in the back alleys normally have the absolute best food. Don't miss out on the local stuff -- figure out how the locals do it and try it out.

Mike B. - Studied in Europe

What do you wish you would have known before you left to study abroad?

The first thing that comes to mind is that I wish I would have planned ahead, and bought plane tickets to fly around Europe on the weekends when I didn't have class. Before I left, I figured I would plan it when I got there. But to buy a plane ticket the week before you want to go is really not worth it if you're just staying for the weekend. So I still feel like if I would of looked into buying tickets a couple of months prior to leaving... I would of been able to get some very cheap tickets, and thus seen more of the world.

What advice would you give someone if they wanted to really maximize their experience?

I would suggest researching the area that you are staying in before you leave. Find out what there is to see, eat, and do there. I bought a guidebook and I used it on a daily basis. Another thing I would suggest is to talk to your teachers in your classes. You need to remember that they themselves are locals and know what is good for the most part. Besides that, I would just say don't turn on the TV once. I had a roommate who stayed inside for the most part and watched movies. We got him to come out more by the end of the trip, but he even said he regretted doing that in the beginning.

Any useful tips for a student studying abroad today?

Just walk around the city you're in. It may seem like no big deal after being there for awhile. But when you come home you well miss that the most. Make sure you do everything you even *might* want to do, I came home with a couple of things that I didn't get to do and it bothers me everyday. Also try to get Euros in the U.S. and bring them. There will be less taxes and charges involved.

What are some things they should they try to avoid?

Avoid going out with more then fifty euros on you unless you know that you are trying to spend more then that. Also try to have people with you when you're walking around. Never walk alone at night, I got pick-pocketed and ended up fighting a guy to get my wallet back. If my roommates weren't there, I don't know what I would of done. For the most part don't talk to strangers at night, never tell anybody were you are staying. Also never write your address on your key, a girl in our program did that and lost her key. Then got robbed two days later. *oops.*

Jack E. - <u>Studied in: Europe and Japan</u>

What do you wish you would have known before you left to study abroad?
The first thing I would say is that culture shock is very real. While some people experience it in different ways... and it varies depending on the place, trying to ignore it is silly. Instead, I would say just embrace the weird changes in mood and mental state, and understand that any negative feelings about your abroad or home country are just a response to being in a new place. I would say that in Japan this was a really important realization. I noticed some subtle changes in my perspective and mood about two and a half months in- after the initial moments of awe wore off. Once I understood

that my mind was treading new cultural tracks, and that this was just part of the process of becoming a self-aware individual, everything sort of fit together.

What advice would you give someone if they wanted to really maximize their experience?

Talking to the locals is a must. If you really want to maximize your experience, learn a few phrases, and be respectful to your host country. Humor seems to be a pretty universal language too. I remember hitchhiking home in Japan after all the trains had stopped for the night. I managed to strike up a conversation with a guy who fell asleep on the train like me. We both realized how screwed we were, and his father-in-law ended up giving us both a ride home because we had shared a laugh together.

Any useful tips for a student studying abroad today?

Pack light, expect things to go wrong, and just go out and travel.

What are some things they should they try to avoid?

This is a tough one, but I would say try and stay away from any sort of activity that could end up with police or mafia. I know a guy who knocked over a Yakuza's motorcycle and had to pay tons of money and was almost deported. And be careful of street food involving meat. It is delicious, but be prepared for the consequences!

Appendix B - Miscellaneous

A compilation of crazy, sometimes unfortunate, but always authentic... Chinese Events: Arrive in Beijing (overwhelming- like Egypt), Angry cab drive through Hutongs, relentless pollution, greetings at Leo Courtyard hostel with free beers, Searching for *Quijode Restaurant- "the Greatest Roast Duck in Asia"*, finding out how much I don't like roast duck, The Great Wall of China's most treacherous section- Simitai, Public toilets, The summer palace, the famous Long Corridor, Beihai Park's 800 year history, 1 of 3 "1,000 Places to See Before You Die" Restaurants- Fangshou, People always asking to take pictures of us and pose, The Forbidden City- beggars galore, man singing opera with his dog on a bicycle, 17 hour train to Xi'an, hard seats, 45 Yuan discount for Terracotta Warriors, accidently cheating a cab driver, Shangyun hostel, hippie's cat eating our omelets. (Xi'an- previously the capitol of China; full of prosperity and wealth... now it's an awful smelling pit). Muslim buffets in Xi'an, closest call of my life- almost missing our train to Shanghai- we only made it because we are American, dirtiest hospitals imaginable, 16 hour train ride to Shanghai, famous Koala Garden Hostel in Shanghai, Old Town Sushi express, famous Nan Xiang steamed buns Restaurant, Best dumpling in the world- according to Anthony Bourdain ~ we respectfully disagreed, motorcycle carriage ride home for 40 Yuan, Jin Mao Tower, Cloud 9 Bar with 18 year old scotch- 87th floor, Grand Hyatt Hotel, Hong Dong Korean restaurant, cucumber juice bar, French Concession wine tasting, Tai Chi with locals in Fuxing Park, Shanghai Expo 2010, The city of Shanghai is like a psychedelic light show that won't stop, Art museum fountain, endless tour buses, 3 hour train ride to Hangzhou, 4 Eyes Hostel- no door on our room, Bikes on West Lake, Teppanyaki all-you-can-eat sushi and steak for 158 Yuan, Dairy Queen and Sake, Flight to Guilin, Happy Hotel, ChinaVoice language program in Beijing costs ½ the price and it's double the time of Rome, People always staring at my big feet, leaving A-list restaurants after food arrived, famous Li River Cruise, Riverside Hostel, picked up at airport at 2 AM- very creepy driver, Tour bus- herded around like camels, 4 hour YanSuo boat ride, best coffee on earth- made with melon, conversations with Alabama man, snake liquor, Flight to Hong Kong, pep talk- we're not gonna take it anymore!, Nasty Garden Lee Hostel, Food at 7/11- very good, endless reflexology shops, prostitutes, Macau Tower Bungee Jump- Highest in the world, Ferry ride to Macau, Bungee master from Detroit- we got ahead of the hours-long line, 233 meter free fall, free beer and slot machines post jump, security guard warning us about getting killed at the Big Buddah- but going anyway, realizing the USA is better than I ever imagined, Hotel Intercontinental Hong Kong- penthouse suite- for free upgrade- treated like Kings, most famous skyline view in Asia- from the Jacuzzi to midnight workout before departure, I picked up the phone to order room service- before I can dial someone on the other line says "what can we do for you Mr. LaVallie and Mr. O'Bryan?"- I've never had service like that for so cheap, truly a trip of a lifetime!

Some quotes overheard and documented while in China-

"China taunts one with its sheer size, it's age, it's depth, and variety... it's unknowable in a single lifetime"

"The Chinese are the most hospitable, respectful, appreciative, and often eccentric as they come. However beyond basic survival instincts, I don't know what keeps them going each day. Vitality is scarce in this super polluted, communist controlled region, and if you don't have a good imagination, the whole country can... sort of feel like a washed up Disneyland."

"Every time we thought something was way too expensive... we would justify it by saying... "Ah, come on... This is like a cheap date at Morton's steakhouse"

"From now on, when people ask me if I should go to China, I would say... just go to Epcot Center... it would eliminate a lot of aggravation... But that's the point!"

"The mystique of China's ancient past is quickly lost through the faces of peasants, beggars, and scammers... as they eagerly shed their dignity for a couple of Yuan."

"Our traveling is like one big puzzle and no matter how out of place everything seems... all the pieces somehow end up falling into place"

"From the Hutongs of Beijing to the Tower of Macau... we have accomplished our mission in understanding the eccentric cultures of the Far East... exploring all of China's major cities and villages... and most importantly- taking a step back and forcing retreat from any form of comfort within these communist borders"

This was a random blog post from one of the pre-arranged trips I took with Loyola Chicago to Sicily: This weekend I went on the Sicily study trip with school, which was a dramatic change of pace compared to most of our excursions that have been completely planned on our own. I was kidding myself though; traveling like this is and always will be an awesome challenge. We took a train from Termini to Naples, which is supposedly the most dangerous city in the world (our cab driver was trying to scare us I think ha-ha)

We power walked through the town, where many people bought 50-cent doughnuts and crepes... until we got to our Ferry that would eventually bring us to Sicily. This so called Ferry was actually a huge cargo ship, and we were forced to dodge swinging I-beams and loaders coming in and out of the ship's exits. I was one of maybe five people who actually bought a room on the enormous ship... I checked in, got my key and went to my room where I found four beds and my own bathroom. This was all very cheap I might add, definitely worth it for an overnight ride to Sicily. Everyone else avoided getting a room because they were worried about having to share it with a Sicilian truck driver, or something similar. Of course this never happened, and I ended up sharing my room with five other people!

Most students were famished from the extreme rush we were in after arriving in Termini, since the only food they had were doughnuts from the street vendors. I won't go into too much detail, but most people thought the food we got was not the best... unless you like anchovies and sardines- which I actually do. That night the thirty of us all made our way to the top of the Ferry towards the bar and dance floor. We had some beer and danced until 2 AM- the teacher who took us on the trip said we were the best Sicily class he's ever had... this same teacher is also one of the most likable guys I've ever met, and also just finished his second Ph.D. from Oxford, so we were in good hands.

We were awoken four hours later and boarded the bus to our first hotel. The main attractions in Sicily were the famous temples of the Gods/Goddesses Zeus, Hercules, and Hera. I took over three hundred pictures in all as this trip was much more of a guided tour from our teacher with everything taken care of for us from food to lodging. We went to top-notch restaurants and I definitely developed some strong friendships here with the extra time we were awarded... not having to worry about the next place we had to see was a nice change of pace.

The second hotel we stayed at was a seaside resort in the town of Taormina, Sicily. Talk about the most beautiful weather, scenery, and beaches you've ever seen... that was Taormina. The hotel was made almost entirely of glass so everywhere you went inside; you had a view of the coastline. Our room had a balcony that was twice the size of the actual living space, and the bathroom had a shower with great water pressure. This is a luxury I have come to endear.

That night we had dinner in the middle of this narrow Carnival-lit up town, there was confetti coming down everywhere in celebration for Carnivale- or the "classy mardi gras" as we like to call it. This place was a true hole-in-the-wall joint with a small dining room that just barely had the means to accommodate us all. Sean and I found the best table in the middle of the room across from our teacher and with some of our best friends. I was right next to a kid named Kevin, who is easily the most well liked kid in our Rome campus. I honestly cannot describe this kid's personality, he's a smaller guy- never has a negative thing to say, knows everyone's first and last name (all 140), always in high spirits... you could be having the worst day of your life and if you cross paths with this kid, you immediately forgot anything that may have been bothering you. But our teacher bought him a glass of grappa after dinner and the whole place joined in his misery when he tried to drink it. We all watched hesitantly and laughed uncontrollably at the poor guy's reaction to grappa. Not the best choice for a first taste of alcohol!

We went to an awesome Irish bar that reminded me of *Ballydoyle Irish Pub in Chicago*. We danced again all night, had the best time... the Sicilians are also some of the most friendly and respectful people I've ever come across. The next day we watched Mount Etna spew some lava from top of a 6th Century BC theatre. My camera battery died at this point, and Sean's broke in six pieces so we didn't capture that, but we had enough pictures from the whole experience on the island. We all shopped a little in the town (2 t-shirts for 10 euro!) and had the best lunch to date before we left. Antipasti of artichokes and cod fillets stood out above the rest. I never thought I would be in a place like Sicily with so many Loyola friends and teachers; it's such a unique and fun experience to be a part of. Many new friends were made and lessons learned in Taormina, Sicily.

End of the year speech

As humans, I believe we all have the *need* to feel like we're constantly growing in some way. Whether it's spiritually, emotionally, physically, or intellectually — we must recognize continual, positive changes in our lives so that we can contribute beyond ourselves.

Lately, I've heard people conveying their personal feelings about this semester abroad coming to an end. When I hear these various remarks — I immediately revert back to our time together in Sienna and think of myself, along with the emotions and anxieties I had at that time ... the unbelievable amount of uncertainty that laid before us — was unreal.

It takes a lot of courage, whether you know it or not, to take that plunge ... into the unknown for four months of our early adult lives. My hope is that you can look back and identify the person you were in Tuscany and observe, through your unique experiences, the growth that has undoubtedly transpired in all areas of your life.

"Preparing people to live extraordinary lives"— Most of us have seen this, as it's written on the walls throughout Loyola University Chicago. For me, it started out as just an optimistic sentiment; my attitudes changing toward it as often as the weather. But since living here in Rome at the John Felice Rome Center with all of you, my outlook has evolved, and these words have become a conviction. I know now, when you recognize this phrase you will feel the same. The stage is set, you have the tools, now use that newfound confidence you've gained in your life — and lead an extraordinary life. Thank you.

281

Notes and Links

(W-curve for culture shock- http://cms.colum.edu/ studentnews/2009/08/ the_wcurve_enjoy_the_honeymoon.php)

http://www.ryanair.com- Book cheap flight quickly and easily.

http://www.hostelworld.com- Reviews, ratings, and easy booking for your next trip.

http://www.skype.com- Communicate with family and friends back home.

www.weatherbase.com- Check the weather conditions everywhere you travel.

http://www.goabroad.com- Travel and study opportunities abroad. Sign up for their newsletter for weekly updates.

http://travel.state.gov- Register with the local embassy and stay safe abroad.

www.YouTube.com- Watch shows like *No Reservations* on the Travel Channel to get you in the mood.

www.StudyAbroadFunding.org- Search your options for financial opportunities.

www.InternationalScholarships.com- Search your options for scholarships.

http://www.internationalsos.com/en/- Explore your options for staying safe and getting the assistance you need overseas.

http://www.travelassistance.com/- Explore your options for staying safe and getting the assistance you need overseas.

www.bodybuilding.com/exercises- Learn how to perform any exercise in the gym to help you stay healthy while you're abroad.

http://www.china.org.cn/english/features/beijing/31300.htm - Read more about Beijing Peking Roast Duck.

http://matadornetwork.com/pulse/1-of-american-students-study-abroad/ - Learn more about current study abroad statistics.

http://live.regnumchristi.org/2011/11/scala-santa/- Learn more about the Holy Stairs we visited in Rome.

http://en.wikipedia.org/wiki/Simatai - For historical facts about the Great Wall destination, Simatai.

http://www.mwtb.org/site/moments-for-you/back-issues/second-quarter-2002/martin-luthers-text.html - Learn more about Marin Luther's historic visit to Rome.

http://www.frodolivesin.us/Catholicwork/id146.htm - Learn more about Sean's experiences with the Catholic Imagination.

http://www.roadtoitaly.com/travel-tips-weather.html - If you plan to spend any time in Italy, make sure to stay up on the weather!

Places of Interest:

The best restaurant we came across in China:
Shanhe Teppanyaki, 137 East Huangcheng Road,
Shanghai, China

The best restaurant we came across in Paris. Outstanding view of the Eiffel Tower: Café de l'Homme, 17, Place du Trocadero et 11 Novembre, 75016 Paris, France

The best meal we had in Rome. This is an authentic Roman gem few people know about due to it's mysterious location and signage:
Felice a Testaccio Via Mastro Giorgio, 29 00153 Roma

For an unmatched view of downtown Shanghai. Have a drink and talk about what's good in life with your best friends:
Cloud 9, Jin Mao Tower, 88 Century Boulevard, Shanghai, China

Other References

Schultz, Patricia. *1000 Places to See before You Die.* New York: Workman, 2003. Print.

"The Secret (2006 Film)." *Wikipedia.* Wikimedia Foundation, 31 July 2012. Web. 01 Aug. 2012.

And a Special Thanks to:

Nellie Rose O'Bryan

For without you, Trento would not have been possible.

Un bacio.

Made in the USA
Middletown, DE
15 December 2015